"If you are a busy person who lov
visitation, this book is for you. It co
clear manner and offers creative ideas for those times when the
ones being visited become bored or feel their life no longer has
meaning. Filled with inspiring stories, it is a valuable tool for
training visitation volunteers."
-Perrie J. Peverall, Abbotsford, BC, Formerly a Chaplain for 20 years with
Fraser Health Authority

"An excellent resource for pastors, parish nurses/faith community
nurses, and lay visitors, this manual provides creative suggestions
so visitors can make the time they spend memorable and
spiritually rich, for the person they visit as well as for themselves."
-Annette Stixrud, Portland, Oregon, Former Executive Director, Northwest
Parish Nurse Ministries

"This is a helpful and practical guidebook using specific
examples of persons and situations. It includes helpful 'Review at
a Glance' charts at chapter endings and questions for visitors to
consider. It suggests Scriptures to use in meeting spiritual needs
and emphasizes working closely with the visitor's pastor."
-Joyce Erovick, Salem, Oregon, Retired Nurse Educator and Parish Nurse
Advisory Board Member

"I have been visiting for 10 years, and *Visiting Mrs. Morgan* is the
best manual I have seen on this subject. It is
something I can turn to when new
challenges come up. Recently I saw
the need to really observe a
person's appearance and
environment; this manual has a
section that was so helpful for
that. There are so many other
ideas here to make visiting a
fun experience and a
blessing."
-Kathy Hull, Dallas, Oregon

Visiting Mrs. Morgan

A Handbook for Visiting Aging, Homebound and Hospitalized People

Julia Quiring Emblen, MN, PhD

Mill Lake Books

Judson Lake House
PUBLISHERS

Copyright © 2014 by Julia Quiring Emblen

All rights reserved. No part of this book may be
reproduced in any form without written permission,
except for brief quotations in critical reviews.

Published by
Mill Lake Books
An imprint of Judson Lake House Publishers
Abbotsford, B.C.

Printed by Lightning Source
Distributed by Ingram

Unless otherwise noted, Scripture quotations are
from The Holy Bible, New International Version®,
NIV®. Copyright © 1973, 1978, 1984, 2011 by Biblica,
Inc.® Used by permission. All rights reserved
worldwide.

ISBN: 978-0-9881462-3-5

Dedication

I would like to dedicate this handbook to my Aunt Tina who never knew the inspiration she provided me as I spent hours on Saturdays helping her cook, bake, clean house, prepare crafts and sewing and knitting handwork. At 45 Aunt Tina contracted polio and that left her paralyzed from the waist down. She learned to walk with braces and wrist crutches, but this never was a very easy endeavor for her.

Initially she had many visitors for she had been an active member in the church, preparing flowers and food for many events. She was especially involved in the Ladies Missionary Sewing Circle. But after the first months and then the 20 years when she was not able to get out to church, the visits decreased and by the time of her death she had visits primarily from family and the paid Pastor to Seniors.

From Aunt Tina I learned about the struggles and the long lonely hours. She never talked about this, but often her sighs and her sad facial expressions told me that she missed the days when she could walk around and go when and where as she pleased.

In order to relieve present homebound of a few of those lonely hours that my Aunt experienced, I have prepared these materials to guide visitors who now volunteer to do homebound visits with additional background, knowledge and skills to increase the effectiveness of these visits.

Acknowledgements

I would especially like to thank my Mother who has read countless drafts, edited, and reread chapters. Mother's guidance is always "write in words people understand" and I have tried to do this.

Pastor Clyde Goin has served as consultant for the chapter on death of the homebound person and visitor coping. He suggested scriptures and ways visitors might learn to relate to those who are dying. He also gave suggestions for visitors to help them cope when the homebound person dies.

Lynn Swedberg, occupational therapist, provided suggestions for content organization and assessment of the abilities of the homebound. She identified some activities that visitors might use to engage the homebound person.

My psychologist nephew, Jason Quiring, reviewed the encouragement chapter for details related to despair and depression.

I appreciate Gaye Stewart's assistance with the Basket chapter. She spoke and demonstrated how to make beautiful baskets for one of our visitor's group meetings.

David and Betty Giesbrecht came alongside and helped with final content editing and with getting this material published.

I am particularly grateful to God for bringing my friend Claudia into my life at a time when I needed her encouragement and expertise. We met when Claudia came to a homebound visitors meeting at our church. When I was tired of revising materials that I had put together for use with our church visiting group, Claudia encouraged me and offered to read the current revision. She did, made excellent suggestions and then read another corrected copy. To my surprise, one day she offered to format the material for me. I thought she would put it into a nicer style, but her formatting included page layout and even flowers.

Contents

Introduction

When I moved to Dallas so Mother would not be alone, I also returned to the church of my childhood. I was surprised to realize that like Mother, others were also aging. When I didn't find Mrs. Morgan (this and other names have been changed to protect privacy) at church, I learned from Mother that she was living in the local nursing care home. I remembered how busy Mrs. Morgan used to be at church in the ladies mission group, preparing flowers for Sunday services and serving as church custodian with her husband. It surprised me to realize that the span of 40 years I had been away had changed not only Mother and me, but also other members of the church.

As soon as I could I went to see Mrs. Morgan. She still remembered me and was so happy to have a visitor come to talk with her. I found that she now was unable to walk well enough to get to church services alone. She told me that the Pastor to Seniors came by to visit her, but her brother was her only other visitor. As she recounted her long, lonely hours I began to think about how to get more church visitors out to her and others like her. As I became more acquainted with the present church congregation, I found that there were ten others who no longer were able to get to church. Several were in the care home and others lived in their homes, but because of their own or their spouse's illness could not get out to church.

I thought about the church bonds that are created in baptism and communion. When we participate in these we share Christ with all Christians in the faith community. These ties provide life-sustaining spiritual encouragement and hope among us. Spiritual bonds, often communicated by sharing time and activities together, extend beyond the normal social practices of friendship.

I began to ponder ways we might extend these bonds when individuals become homebound. Of course Sunday bulletins and DVD's of the Sunday worship service provided some connection, but the homebound people were truly touched when members of the congregation visited.

My years of working in the community, and most recently my parish nursing experiences, guided my thinking about how to set up meaningful congregational visits. I was sure that, if requested, several people would be willing to visit homebound people on a regular basis. They certainly would provide church news and current events and probably end their visit by reading scripture and praying with the homebound person.

I wondered about other activities the visitor might introduce to help the homebound person cope with the lonesome hours between visits. A visitor could initiate a scripture memory program suited to the homebound person's ability. Some of the conversation might focus on Bible stories and particular people. But visitors could include lots of other activities such as planting an indoor garden, making a bird feeder, designing a reminiscence box, creating a visitor book, reviewing books, organizing photos, etc. Some visitors told me they used music, made baskets (either for or with those they visited), and wrote life stories from the stories their visitees told them.

I soon initiated a group of people to visit the homebound. We met together monthly to describe our visits and special needs and problems that occurred during the visits and we prayed for the needs of those we visited. We talked about a variety of things they did and wanted to begin doing together.

As the visitors recounted their visits they also identified some special skills that would help them be more effective: what to observe during visits; how to encourage and use humor. Some expressed concern about the difficulty of communicating with physically impaired people. Other visitors indicated a need for preparation to deal with the approaching death of the person and their own anticipatory grieving of the loss.

In this manual activities and skills useful in visiting the homebound are organized according to each of the letters in the word "HOMEBOUND." Each chapter includes a brief anecdote illustrating a particular need, some guidelines for using the skill, a review box of key points and questions for personal thought or for discussion if a group of people are involved.

Note: *When referring to a homebound person or care facility resident, the term "visitee" has been adapted in these materials to distinguish the one being visited from the church visitor.*

How to Use This Book

The nine chapters in this handbook have been developed to briefly address the most common activities and the background knowledge that visitors to the homebound need in order to make their visits meaningful and useful.

Why would a person need this information? Homebound people are often very lonely. This is not only because they are forgotten by their friends when they are unable to get out to church services or other events for months or even years. The homebound person also has fewer visits due to the uncertainty that potential visitors feel. Visitors aren't sure how to relate to people who have become so different as they attempt to cope with physical and other changes arising from the ravages of their chronic illnesses. As a result, visitors are afraid they might say or do something that would be hurtful. Instead, they send flowers or cards. Or they stop in for a short time to read a few verses from the Bible, pray, and leave as quickly as they can—commenting about not wanting to tire the homebound person. But the quick departure often is because the visitor does not know what else to do and has run out of friendly conversation topics.

The materials in this book have been designed to provide some insight regarding key problems that the visitor is likely to encounter. They also offer some suggestions about how the visitor might effectively interact during the visit to express true caring and active Christian love. The goal of each chapter is to help the visitor make every visit special and memorable, providing encouragement and fun to the person or family being visited.

Who is the target audience for the handbook? This handbook is intended for people who visit someone who is confined due to illness in a hospital, home, nursing home, or other caregiving facility. These visitors may include pastors, chaplains, deacons, elders, church members, and friends.

How can the handbook best be used? Anyone can read it at his/her own pace. The best context would be to use this book as the reference handbook for a 10-week group discussion. Each week the focus would be on one chapter. It will work best if the participants are making visits during this time so they can practice using some of the suggestions in each chapter and come back the next week to share their experiences with the group. The final week could be a review and summary, as members encourage each other in their service of visiting the homebound.

This handbook could also be taken to the visit in addition to a Bible if the visitor chooses to bring one. Appendix A offers resources for eight focus areas or situations that visitors may encounter: three are positive experiences, four are common difficulties, and the eighth is the need for salvation. The discussion of each area includes an anecdote to help identify the context in which that situation might arise, followed by relevant Bible verses and a sample prayer. (In a group discussion, participants might add other focus areas that have arisen in their visits and ask group members to help identify relevant scriptures and prayer petitions that might be used in subsequent conversations.)

It is best if each person retains a copy of the handbook as a personal resource. Perhaps a church or other umbrella group might consider supplying copies to those choosing to serve as visitors to homebound people. Several churches might combine, so that the visitors from the various churches could come together for a weekly discussion focused around the content included in the handbook.

Chapter One

Humor

Suggestions for Introducing Humor During a Visit

Illustrations of the Use of Humor in Visits

Rita and Susan

Susan related a happy thought to Rita—"My snoring makes the lady in the next room sleep better! It reminds her of her husband's snoring." Thinking of it, Susan laughed heartily—exercising all of her internal organs with her belly laugh.

Then she commented in a serious voice, "Sometimes I wonder what I'm good for anymore. I just sit here every day—I can't do much of anything. But then God showed me that He can even use my snoring to help others."

Rita said that she enjoys her visits with Susan because she is usually happy. She laughs and smiles a lot, unlike

"A cheerful
heart is
good medicine."
Proverbs 17:22

some visitees who give the impression they have just bitten into a lemon. Rita knew that Susan had pain and dealt with immobility, but she related to these with her positive sense of humor. Rita realized that humor helps people forget some of their daily struggles for a few moments of time.

Guidelines for Using Humor

"Did you hear about the man who read the sign on our door?" the florist clerk asked. "It reads 'Say it with flowers.' He came in and asked me to wrap up one red rose. When I asked, 'Only one?' he responded, 'I'm a man of few words.'"

Did you laugh at that joke? Maybe you did—some of you may have cried, wanting a few more roses. How do you think your visitee would respond to this joke? In using humor, the trick is to tell stories or report anecdotes that appeal to and make the person respond with a big belly laugh. That's one aspect that is so healthy about humor—it exercises many of the internal organs.

Four Functions of Humor:

Internal Jogging Especially for those who have limited mobility, a good belly laugh can serve to exercise the abdomen, intestines and lungs—similar to the action that occurs when a person jogs.

Psychological Effect When a person laughs, this activity serves to help the person's body and reduce general tension. Relaxation is a major function of humor.

Sociological Effect When people laugh together, they usually forget their individual role and status differences. Laughter becomes a natural way to equalize or reduce individual differences of members of a group.

Spiritual Transcendence When people are physically moved, they are transported to another place. In some situations related to illness or crisis, it is not possible to move persons, but they can move their mental focus from the situation to something else. Crisis situations, tragedies, and chronic illness may be lightened, at least for a few moments, when some meaningful humor is introduced. Spiritual transcendence helps the person mentally move beyond the painful experience.

Humor Points

True humor is more than simply telling a joke. For those of us who often forget the punch-line, this may be a comfort. Humor actually combines funny details as well as a certain presence of mind. The French expression *jeu d'espirit* captures the idea that humor involves mind transcendence. The literal meaning is "game of the mind" or wit. Witty jokes are often equated with humor, but the joke is only one of the vehicles to achieve the purpose of mind transcendence.

A funny face identifies some key points of humor. True humor generates warmth, delight, exuberance and other positive responses which are communicated through non-verbal glances or by words. Sometimes humor presents unexpected happy surprises, fun and comic activities. The sensation produced by humor changes negatively or neutrally charged emotional tones and serves to lighten one's spirits.

Definition: Humor is a spontaneous response that promotes health through positive communication that helps decrease negative thoughts and responses.

This little funny face depicts key components of humor.

PROMOTE POSITIVE

Comic

Emotions

Fun

Laughter

RELEASE NEGATIVE

Suggestions for using humor with visitee:

1. Collect comic strip cartoons to share with visitees. Share one at every visit.

2. Keep eyes open to see the funny things happening in everyday life.

3. Discover the elf in your<u>self</u>. (Elves often are characterized by silly behavior.)

4. Share the funniest thing that ever happened and ask visitee to share funniest thing.

5. Use real life events like Susan's snoring and turn it into something funny and meaningful as Susan did.

6. Make an acrostic using the letters in the word laughter.

Sample of LAUGHTER acrostic

L ove one another

A nticipate fun

U nderstand different views of human beings

G rin

H um a happy tune

T hink of the positives

E njoy people and things around you

R elax

Try making an acrostic with your visitee for LAUGHTER.

Review at a Glance

Original Humor	Helpful Types	Activities	Functions
Comments people make Preplanned • Funny face • Cartoons • Joke books	Cartoon comics Animal adventures Proverbs Riddles	Make an acrostic from the word laughter. Collect comic strips that fit homebound person's life or situation. Discover the ELF in yourself. Notice funny signs or happenings right around you.	Physiological-internal jogging Psychological-relaxation Sociological-natural equalizer Spiritual transcendence • Facilitates mental movement beyond painful experience • Lightens heaviness of chronic illness • Strengthens faith and trust

Questions

1. How does your definition of humor compare with the one given?

2. Why are the examples of humor different for Susan than ones you would relate to?

3. How does humor help a person?

4. What are some of the physiological, psychological and spiritual functions of humor?

5. What do you think about the comment that 'true humor goes beyond remembering the punch line of a joke'?

6. How could you plan to introduce some type of humor during your next homebound visit?

Chapter Two

Observation of Person and Environment

Areas to Assess When Visiting

By observing the person and the environment
the visitor can learn very important information

Illustrations of Physical Observations

Bill and Todd

One afternoon when Bill stopped to visit Todd he found
him awake, but he looked awful. His finger tips were dusky
blue and purple tinged. Todd invited Bill in, but his effort to
get up to open the door left him gasping for breath. He sort
of coughed and attempted to smile, but it turned out to be
only a grimace. Without even thinking, Bill burst out, "Todd,

"Why does your face
look so sad when
you are not ill?
This can be nothing
but sadness of heart."

Nehemiah 2:2

what's wrong?" And then he noticed that Todd's usual oxygen tank was beside his chair, but he didn't have that small plastic tube in his nose.

"Oxygen tank is empty," Todd responded between gasps.

Even though Bill hated to have him talk because he was so short of breath, Todd told him that the usual company that replaced his oxygen tank had a problem with equipment and they hadn't come that week. Since Todd looked so awful, Bill decided to call the group facilitator of his visiting group to see what he should do. If he couldn't reach her immediately he knew he needed to call 911.

Illustrations of Mental Observation

Lydia and Tonya

Lydia had been visiting with Tonya weekly for several months. She had learned that Tonya had experienced the death of her daughter six months earlier and the loss of her husband two years before. Usually Tonya was quiet so Lydia had tried to keep their conversations light-hearted and usually brought up happy things to talk and think about.

This morning when Tonya opened the door to let her in, she was shocked by the change in Tonya's behavior. Instead of her usual friendly, quiet greeting, Tonya smiled and showed her pleasure with the visit by gushing over Lydia as she walked into the living room. "Oh, I'm so glad to see you! No one but you ever comes to visit me. You're my only real friend!"

"I enjoy visiting you. You and I have things in common that we both enjoy. Have you been doing some more work on your travel scrap book?" Lydia asked.

"Oh yes, I have done a lot," Tonya held it out pointing to only the old pictures that had been previously put in. "I've included pictures of our trip to Hawaii and then I added pictures from our Mexican trip," Tonya held out envelopes of pictures that didn't appear to even be opened.

"But Tonya, you haven't even looked at these sets of pictures. The envelopes are still sealed," Lydia protested. "You had these pictures of New York City in here when I looked at the book several weeks ago."

"Oh, I have just been so busy—I haven't had time to paste them in," Tonya interrupted. "I've been entertaining many guests. You know the Blacks? They live next door. They were here for dinner last night and my son and his family came the day before."

Lydia realized that something was wrong with Tonya. She was making up such wild tales. Tonya's son lived two states away and on a previous visit Tonya had said her son only came to see her at Christmas time.

Lydia tried once more, "Tonya, are you feeling all right?"

"Oh, yes, I'm so excited to have you come. It's so good that we have things to talk about. Let me tell you about my shopping trip yesterday..."

Lydia let Tonya prattle on as she pondered what to do. Should she call the pastor? Maybe she should call the facilitator of the visiting program. Lydia remembered that in her visiting group they had recently had a discussion on what was termed "mood swings" that people who are alone sometimes have.

She knew that Tonya definitely was behaving and talking differently. Usually they had a nice quiet conversation and Tonya always thanked her for visiting. But today Tonya's exuberance and tall tales were obviously fabricated.

When she left Tonya, Lydia picked up her cell phone and was relieved when Ruth, the visit facilitator, answered. She explained how she had found Tonya and Ruth said it was good that Lydia had called. Ruth knew how to reach Tonya's son and she said she would contact him immediately. Ruth agreed with Lydia's impression that Tonya's obvious mood swing needed to be checked out more fully. Perhaps she needed some medication, or maybe Tonya had forgotten to take her usual medications. Either of the possibilities could account for Tonya's unusual behavior.

Guidelines for Personal Observation

You **must** also include observation of possible abuse/ neglect that are **urgent** personal needs and the church office **must** be notified immediately if visitor notes any of the first three observations:

- Visitee acts fearful, or expresses fear of caregiver or family members
- Recent bruises or injuries
- Visitee left alone who cannot exit home independently

Because the next three observations are not life-threatening, the facilitator of the visitation group should be notified as soon as possible:

- Paid caregivers not performing their duties
- Person not clean, wearing soiled clothes
- Visitee reports giving small amounts of money away, e.g. to new neighbor or friend

Review at a Glance

Observations of Person*

Physical	Face
	Is skin dry? Moist?
	Are there dark circles under eyes?
	Color
	Is skin pale, blue, yellow?
	Are eyeballs yellow, red?
	Are nail beds pale?
	Mobility
	Does person move quickly, slowly?
	Can person use walker, wheelchair?
	Does person remain in bed?
	Comfort
	Is person at ease, restful?
	Does person express pain with certain movements?
	Is person constantly in pain?
	Abuse/neglect (<u>urgent</u>, report immediately)
	Bruises on face or arms
	Fresh wounds on body
Mental	**Attitude**
	Is person generally upbeat?
	Is person generally discouraged?
	Affect
	Is person able to express feelings?
	Are feelings expressed appropriate to the conversation?

*These may not all be noted on every visit, but they suggest areas to observe.

Questions (for Observation of Persons)

1. What can a visitor observe about a homebound person?

2. Which area is easier to observe—physical or mental?

3. Why are these observations important?

4. Who should observe the homebound to identify personal needs?

Illustrations of Environmental Observations

"...And bring me, please, a piece of bread."
"As surely as the Lord your God lives," she
replied, "I don't have any bread—only a handful of
flour in a jar and a little oil in a jug. I am gathering a
few sticks to take home and make a meal for myself
and my son, that we may eat it—and die."

I Kings 17:11-12

Frances and Lillian

Frances, a fairly new visitor, arrived at Lillian's home late one Thursday afternoon. As she drove up she was surprised that the house was dark. She noted that she had to dodge branches from several shrubs to get up the steps to ring the doorbell. While she waited to see if Lillian was home she glanced around checking for loose railings and step stability. She made a mental note to ask the homebound coordinator if anyone from church was available to do yard work.

Responding to the doorbell, Lillian invited Frances in. "It's dark so early now that we are back onto Standard time. Shall I turn the light on?" Frances asked.

"I wish you could," Lillian sighed. "This morning I turned on the light because the clouds and rain make it so dark. The light bulb flashed and burned out. When I looked for another one, there weren't any in the package. Maybe that was good, because it is hard for me to reach up to the light socket to replace it."

"Oh, I could go to the store to get some bulbs and then screw one into a socket for you," Frances volunteered.

"But I don't want to bother you. We could visit in the dark. I will ask my neighbor to get some bulbs a little later in the week." Lillian was hesitant about accepting Frances' offer of help.

Frances found another lamp that she could turn on and then sat down to visit with Lillian. As they talked, it occurred to her that Lillian might be out of other things too. She had also noted that the room was quite cool. Perhaps her social security check was late or didn't cover all the expenses this month. She wondered how she could find out. When Lillian had a coughing spell Frances offered to get her some juice or something to drink. "Is your juice in the refrigerator?"

When Lillian nodded between coughing gasps, Frances went to the kitchen and after picking up a glass she opened the refrigerator and found one small half empty juice can. She also noticed that there was no milk and there were few fresh fruits or vegetables stored in the refrigerator. There were only a small bowl of what looked like chili and a few slices of bread on the frig shelf. The kitchen sink was cluttered and dirty dishes were scattered all over the counter. She also noticed that a pile of laundry was on the floor beside the washer that was located near the back door.

Frances was not quite sure what to do about these things. She felt at a loss to address the cleaning and laundry issues. And oh yes, there was a loose cord in the living room that could easily cause a fall. She was glad there were no scatter rugs around. She added the cleaning, laundry and loose cord to her mental list.

She decided that she needed to be direct with her

visitee about groceries. She knew that Lillian could not get out for groceries due to her bad knees. But she had understood that someone brought in food and other household supplies.

"Here's the last of that can of juice," she said as she handed the glass to Lillian. After Lillian took a few sips and when she had a chance to catch her breath, Frances continued. "I thought that your neighbor picked up groceries and things for you—I didn't see much in the refrigerator for your dinner tonight."

"Oh I usually just open a can of something. It is too much work for me to cook some days. My neighbor has been sick this week, so he didn't get out for groceries. I guess my cupboards are a little bare. Maybe that's good. I can afford to lose a little weight—easier for me to get around." Lillian looked embarrassed.

"Well, I'd be happy to get some groceries for you, and light bulbs."

As she went to her car she also thought about Lillian's decreasing mobility. Since there were no smoke detectors that she could see, she wondered how Lillian would be able to recognize a fire and then get out of her home. She decided to get the groceries and then call the group facilitator immediately.

Guidelines for Personal and Environmental Observations

Visitors should not snoop around the house and invade the visitee's personal areas. Rather, they should just be observant and note areas that seemed to be concerns while normally visiting. Visitors can observe both visually and by smell any evidence of a small fire: pot with burned on food or stove burners not turned off. This is an **urgent** environmental need and if observed should immediately be reported to the facilitator of visiting group or to the church secretary.

Guidelines for Visitor Action Regarding Special Needs

Visitors should call group facilitator regarding special environmental needs. Facilitator will make contacts with person and family regarding the need. Possibly a 'circle of caring' group may need to be created so that volunteers can be coordinated to assist as needed with installing household safety devices, etc. Additional community resources can be contacted by facilitator. Facilitator may discuss Criteria for Lifeline or similar emergency call system with family.

Call 911 if the situation visitor encounters is a personal or an environmental emergency that is potentially life threatening.

Review at a Glance

Observation of Environment

Appearance	• Is the area colorful? • Is the room light? • What style is the furniture? • Are there pictures? • Are there flowers or plants? • Are there greeting cards around? • Themes of cards—encouraging, religious • Number of cards—few or many? • Are there knick knacks around? • Are there other things that provide cues as to hobbies?
Supplies	• Is there enough food—milk, bread, fruits, etc.? • Does the person have enough medications for pain, cough, etc.? • Are there enough household supplies around like light bulbs, soap, tissues, etc.?
Space	**Safety** • Are there leaky faucets? • Are there cords across areas where person walks? • Are there loose objects around that could create walking hazards? • Are there small scatter rugs that slip? • Is there recent evidence of small fire, pot with burned food or stove burners left on? (<u>Urgent</u> Need--call immediately) • Person fearful of neighborhood, reports of possible harassment • Malfunctioning locks on doors/windows • Icy sidewalks, not shoveled • Lack of handrails, grab bars, other needed safety features **Convenience** • Is the furniture arranged to allow easy movement? • Have modifications been made to accommodate disability—chair up on blocks, ramps rather than stairs? • Can person get up from low chair? **Cleanliness** • Is there clutter around? • Is the area visibly clean?
Temperature	• Is the room too warm/cool? • Can the room temperature be controlled by a thermostat change? Or, is the heating or cooling adjusted in another way?

Questions (for Observation of Environment)

1. Why should a visitor make observations of the visitee's environment?

2. If supplies are low, what could the visitor do about this?

3. If the home looks dirty, what might the visitor do about this?

4. Because convenience with respect to walking is key, how might a visitor get assistance with furniture relocation or small construction projects such as Lillian's home needed?

5. If a room is very hot or very cold, what might be some reasons? How might the visitor help?

6. If you found the kind of situation Frances encountered, whom would you call at your church to provide help?

7. Do you know if there is an emergency assistance fund in your church that might be used for groceries and/or to pay someone to do minor household chores?

Chapter Three

Using Music
as Part of a Visit

Illustrations of the Effects of Music

Barry and Ted

As Barry was walking in to visit Ted he heard the familiar melody of a song he recalled from past years. He stood in the doorway, not wanting to interrupt Ted as he sat in repose. Ted looked peaceful, but he looked up and noticed Barry standing calmly in the doorway. Putting one finger up in the air Ted mouthed the words, "Just one minute."

After the song he was listening to was finished, Ted

"Speak to one another
with psalms, hymns
and spiritual songs.
Sing and make music
in your heart to the
Lord."

Ephesians 5:19

turned off his tape. "Every once in awhile I just have to have some music to lift my spirits. That song always helps."

Barry nodded his head in agreement. "I know what you mean. It is amazing how music affects me. Sometimes I'm just feeling down and I put on a happy tune and bingo! Singing along I begin to feel better."

"My mother was really affected by music even after she was pretty confused. One St. Patrick's Day I visited her when they had a guest pianist. The pianist played the usual Irish songs while mother nodded off with most of the other residents. On inspiration after the pianist finished a song, I asked her if she knew 'The Old Rugged Cross.' She did and as she began playing most of the residents woke up and began singing along. I asked her to play 'Jesus Loves Me' while mother and others sang along," Barry recalled.

Guidelines for Using Music

Definition: Science and art of incorporating pleasing expression or intelligible combinations of tones using rhythm, melody, harmony and counterpoint.

Description of Music Therapy

Music therapy is a scientific and functional application or use of music by a therapist who tries to achieve specific changes in an individual's behavior. This is useful to relieve pain, distract from certain disturbing procedures and to soothe a person's spirit. Sometimes it is useful in drawing people out who are unable to speak, but are still able to sing along with others or to accompaniment.

Sometimes music therapists refer to music as a "musical bath."[1]   Persons are asked to allow themselves to be immersed in the musical sounds thinking of what it feels like to be in a warm relaxing hot tub or under a warm shower. The sound becomes cleansing to the body and calming to emotions just like bath oil in a water bath. The music is allowed to resonate in different parts of the body and the person becomes relaxed and refreshed, calm and balanced.

Using music is usually easy and enjoyable both for visitors and visitees. Visitors need to check with their visitees and when they know the kind of music the visitee likes, the visitor might bring a CD of the style of preference. Possibly the visitee might have some that could be played. Visitors often find that music lifts spirits and visitees might even be able to express themselves more easily while listening to music.

Often confused people respond to songs they have heard in the past. For example, sometimes a Christmas hymn (regardless of whether it is around Christmas) will encourage a confused person to sing along. Sometimes those who have not spoken for years are able to sing the words to old favorite songs and hymns.

Review at a Glance

Music

Definition	Purpose	Scripture Verses	How
Science and art of incorporating pleasing expression or intelligible combinations of tones using rhythm, melody, harmony and counterpoint.	• Decrease anxiety • Increase relaxation • Release tension • Draw people out • Provide sense of transcendence	I Samuel 16:14-23 Psalm 95:1-2 Colossians 3:16	• Sing together • Sing alone • Play tape or CD • Play instrument • Drumming—beating time • Hum • Sing hymns (use large print copies) • Sing ethnic tunes • Use hymns based on scripture as a Bible study

Questions

1. How have you personally, or with someone else, found music decreased anxiety or promoted relaxation?

2. How does music help us to glorify and praise God?

3. Why do you think music draws out even confused people?

4. If you don't sing, besides bringing a CD player and discs, how might you incorporate music into a visit?

[1] Guzzetta, C. E. (1988). Music Therapy: Hearing the melody of the Soul. In Dossey, B.M. (et al.). (Eds.) *Holistic Nursing: A Handbook.* Rockville, Maryland: Aspen Publications.

Chapter Four

Encouragement

Ways to Help Visitees Increase Their Courage

Illustration of Encountering Discouragement

Liz and Adelle

As Liz entered the room she caught sight of Adelle sitting in her wheelchair stooped forward, head bowed with her eyes closed. Liz's heart sank. She wondered how on earth she could encourage someone with all those physical signs of discouragement. But she decided to give it her best try.

"Hi Adelle. I thought that I'd drop by to visit with you this morning," Liz paused, waiting for a response that would show her if her first observation of Adelle's profound discouragement was right.

"An anxious heart weighs a man down, but a kind word cheers him up."
Proverbs 12:25

"Hi," Adelle responded with a deadpan voice, she barely stirred. She didn't even look at Liz.

"Has your week been good?" Liz tried to make her voice sound upbeat.

"So-so," Adelle's facial features appeared frozen. She neither smiled nor frowned.

"Today is St. Patrick's Day. I saw on the bulletin board that a party is scheduled for 2 p.m. Do you think they'll give out shamrocks?" Liz asked trying to get Adelle interested.

"I have no idea. I don't plan to go."

After a few more attempts at conversation Liz went home wondering what else she might have done to encourage Adelle. Liz recalled that after Adelle's stroke she had been in rehab until funds were used up. She had not made enough progress to go back to the apartment she and her husband had shared. She could not manage her care needs by herself. Adelle had a daughter who lived nearby, but she was only able to see her once a week. Adelle could push her wheelchair using her feet, but that took a lot of effort, so she often had to wait for someone to come help her—even to get to the bathroom. Her stroke had made her quite dependent on others. Liz realized that Adelle didn't really have many things occurring in her life experience that were encouraging to her. So Liz decided that she needed to call her group facilitator. After she heard Liz recount her frustrating visit the facilitator promised to focus the next group discussion on encouragement.

Guidelines to Facilitate Encouragement

Definition: Inspire with courage, spirit or hope by heartening and emboldening, helping, supporting; foster attitude or response of facing and dealing with anything recognized as dangerous, difficult or painful instead of withdrawing from it. (Courage is derived from French word which means heart. The heart is the organ that literally pumps blood to all body areas making life possible. Similarly hope and confidence must become part of a person to have the heart or courage to cope with illness and life difficulties.)

1. Encounter

- Sit down at eye level.
- Sit on the whole chair—people sometimes give the impression they only have a little time by sitting on part of the chair.
- Make eye contact—but only if that is comfortable—sometimes people are more comfortable with a side by side orientation, looking out at something together.
- Listen—but also be ready to just sit in silence until the person is ready to talk, forego temptation to fill silence with chatter which a discouraged person may not be up for.

2. Express

Use Reflection

Statement:	"I'm feeling down in the dumps today!"
Reflection:	"You're 'down in the dumps'?"
Response:	"My health insurance does not pay for any more rehab for me. So I'm stuck where I am and don't yet have enough strength in my legs to use a walker."

3. Enable

Thoughts
Events
Words

Demonstrating gentleness is critical in relating to a discouraged person. Probably the sign on the back of the egg truck characterizes the kind of gentleness which is required: 'Hit me <u>gently</u>, I'm full of eggs.' The word <u>eggs</u> could be exchanged with <u>fears</u>. The discouraged person's total body posture, verbal, and non-verbal communication really shouts: **"Treat me gently—I'm full of fears."**

It may help to picture the discouraged person's mind or heart encircled with many fears represented by the circles around the shaded heart in the model. Encouragers must be able to get through those layers of fears by using their heart of love to touch the heart of the one who is so bound by fears.

Pain and anger are emotional experiences that make the heart heavy or discouraged. **Encountering** symptoms of discouragement is easy. The person usually is slumped over in a chair with head bowed and eyes closed. Facial expression is neutral or sad and the person gives terse responses to questions. The goal is to help the person **express** feelings and then **enable** the person to become heartened or enthusiastic about something in life. This enabling usually occurs in three ways—thoughts, events, and words.

A key step in enabling is to help the discouraged person identify more positive ***thoughts***. Sometimes providing hope for something such as planning an activity ahead of time so the person has something to look forward to. It may be helpful for the person to have a reason to get dressed for the day or a special occasion. Focusing on something positive that is happening may be good. A visitor might bring forsythia or pussy willows or the first buttercups to a visit as a sign that the long winter is over and spring is coming.

Sometimes small ***events*** help change a thought. Even a friendly smile and sending or receiving a card or gift can become important avenues of encouragement.

Offer the visitee a chance to serve instead of just receiving from others. Bring cards the visitee can address to friends having birthdays, etc.

__Words__ are probably the most frequent means through which encouragement is fostered. Positive feedback, suggestions for change, promises of prayer and personal affirmation are essential to provide encouragement. Scripture underscores the importance of words:

A word aptly spoken is like apples
of gold in settings of silver.
Proverbs 25:11

Therefore encourage one
another and build each other
up, just as in fact you are doing.
I Thessalonians 5:11

Pleasant words are a
honeycomb, sweet to the soul
and healing to the bones.
Proverbs 16:24

Review at a Glance

Encouragement

Encounter Discouragement	Express	Enable
• Sit at eye level • Sit on the whole chair as if planning to be there for a time • Make eye contact or sit side by side • Listen and/or sit in silence for periods of time	Help person describe fears or anger or whatever has produced discouragement. Use **Reflection**	Approach in a way that will help the discouraged person to face life again by • Demonstrating gentleness • Self-giving • Consistency • Sincere person orientation
Symptoms	**Reflection Technique**	**Techniques to Hearten**
• Stooped posture slumped over in chair • Head bowed • Eyes closed • No facial expression or sad look • Deadpan voice • Brief responses to questions	Repeat key phrase that person makes to draw out more information. **Example--** "I'm feeling down today." "You're 'feeling down'?" "Yes, I can't even tie my own shoe laces anymore."	Replace negative **_thoughts_** with positive ideas. Make time of visit a special **_event_**—bring card, flower or other special treat. Use **_words_** to provide positive feedback, suggest changes, promise to pray and in other ways to provide personal affirmation.

Questions

1. What behaviors have you seen that show discouragement?

2. How did you attempt to modify it?

3. Which of the ideas identified might be especially helpful for your discouraged visitee?

4. Which of the enabling activities for providing encouragement would you find easier to use? Why?

5. How can a visitor change a person's thoughts?

6. How might a visitor set up a special event visitee would enjoy?

7. How does a visitor use words to provide personal affirmation and other positive feedback?

8. What changes in responses do you expect to see when a person becomes more encouraged?

Chapter Five

Baskets of Faith and Fun

Scriptural Basket Discussion and
Ideas for Filling and Decorating Baskets

Illustration of a Faith Basket and How to Prepare a Care Basket

Rita and Susan

Rita was beginning her second six months of visiting Susan. She didn't want her visits to become boring or stale for Susan. She had been pondering what to do to make the visit special when she came across a devotional article. The article by Delores Friesen[1] was titled "Baskets of Faith" and it described three baskets of faith.

The author referred to the basket Jochebed and Amram prepared to put their infant son in as a faith basket.

"Your basket...
will be
blessed."

Deuteronomy 28:5

They undoubtedly sealed it carefully with pitch and other substances to make it waterproof before dispatching it with its precious bundle to float on the Nile River. (Exodus 2:1-10) Friesen commented that this must have taken great courage and compassion as well as faith that God would care for baby Moses. The faith of these parents was honored in a way they probably never anticipated.

Saul (later renamed Paul) was in Damascus when he had to be let down in a basket over the city wall to escape the Jewish leaders waiting at the gate to arrest him for defaulting to Christianity. (Acts 9:17-25) Friesen described this basket as one of hope and willingness to risk for another.

A third faith basket of faith was filled when a mother put a few fish and some barley bread in a basket for a meal as they went to listen to the rabbi who spoke so well. (Matthew 14:15-21) When the disciples called for food her son brought them the little basket of food. One can almost hear the jesting comments about this amount being nothing in terms of feeding 5,000 men along with women and children. But Jesus took the food, gave thanks, and distributed it. When everyone had finished eating they filled 12 baskets with leftovers! The lesson—when we bring what we have to Jesus, we allow Him to bless and expand whatever we bring to Him, for our own as well as the needs of many others.

As Rita read, she suddenly had an inspiration. She could make this a **Faith Basket** time with Susan. Acting on her inspiration, Susan went out to purchase a lovely basket large enough to hold a few things, but not too heavy to carry. To her surprise, the baskets were being sold at half price.

Rita then thought about what she might put into the basket that would be fun and meaningful to Susan. Well, first a lunch could go in that they could have together and ask Jesus to bless. As she thought about a lunch, Rita recalled a basket lunch that Priscilla (a dear friend of her late husband) had brought to her when she was sitting in the hospital waiting room and her husband was down the hall in critical care, barely clinging to life. Priscilla hadn't paid any attention to others in the waiting room, but pulled out a beautiful white table cloth and spread it on the small table in front of the couch. From her basket Priscilla pulled tiny salt and pepper shakers, dainty butter dish and knife, soup, salad, homemade bread and a pie. What a special basket lunch that had been. For those few lunch moments while eating with Priscilla, she had even forgotten how desperately ill her husband was.

Rita put a little less spectacular lunch, just a sandwich and lemonade, into her basket for Susan. At five minutes to twelve, Rita arrived with basket in hand at Susan's door. "Hi Susan, I brought this basket with a little lunch for us today." Rita greeted Susan with a happy smile.

"Oh, I am so glad you came. It will be lovely to have lunch together. It is so hard for me to go out now. The food here is okay, but it isn't anything I'd especially want to share with others." Susan expressed her pleasure over a change of menu.

"Could we use this chair as a table to set our lunch out?" Rita asked pointing to a small table near the couch.

"Sure, that's good. I used to have TV tables that folded up. They would be perfect now."

"This will work just fine." Rita unfolded the large red and white checked napkin on the chair and put the chicken salad sandwiches out along with the little bunches of red grapes.

"Oh, I love chicken salad. I used to make it whenever I made chicken soup," Susan smiled as she helped arrange the food on the table.

"Just minutes ago I squeezed the lemons for our lemonade." Rita dropped ice cubes into the red and white plastic glasses and poured lemonade over them.

"Fresh lemonade. I really like it."

"There, I think we're ready. I'll ask the Lord to bless our food," Rita said as she paused to give Susan time to bow her head.

"Lord, we thank you for this food, we ask you to bless it. Also, be present with us in our conversation. Thank you for letting Susan and me enjoy this meal together. Amen." Rita looked up and was happy to see that Susan was eagerly reaching to pick up her sandwich.

When they had finished their lunch, Rita reached back into her basket and brought out a mini basket with a bright yellow ribbon. "Susan, I brought this little basket to leave here with you. It is small, so it won't take up much room. I read about faith baskets in the Bible—the one baby Moses was put into to float on the river at the time the Pharaoh had decreed that the babies be killed, the one used to lower Saul when the Jews wanted to kill him for becoming a Christian, and the little food basket the boy brought to Jesus. These three baskets represent the faith that the people who used them had. How would it be if we each keep a little basket (I have one at home) and write on a little piece of paper a special need that we want to bring to the Lord along with our faith that He will meet the need?" Rita paused to see if Susan was interested in doing this.

"I think that would be a good idea. I guess I shouldn't have any needs anymore, but it always seems as if something comes up—like my swollen ankles," Susan admitted apologetically.

"God knows each of us and that our needs vary at every phase of life. I have needs too. Being retired, I want to know how God is leading me to serve Him."

"Maybe we could talk over how God is working with our needs whenever you come," Susan suggested.

"Oh, Susan, that would be great. Every time I come to visit I want to bring back this bigger basket that I brought our lunch in today." Rita looked at Susan to see if she was following this idea.

"We'll have our <u>big</u> basket and our <u>little</u> basket of <u>faith</u>," Susan expressed strong conviction and delight over the idea of using a basket to share things.

How to Put a Gift Basket Together

Select a Basket

Select basket size and shape according to basket recipient
- Women—heart shaped might be nice for jewelry.
- Men—Shoe box or other shape wrapped with comics or sports page.

Be sure basket size is such that things overflow the top.

Basket Preparation
Get filler for bottom—shredded paper, crushed tissue paper, florist "hay".

Arrange items so they face towards the front.

Cut cellophane in the shape of a square, so it will wrap around the entire basket, about 6 inches longer than basket handle or things in basket. Gather up cellophane to the top of the basket.

Secure with the bow. See the next page to learn how to make a bow.
Scotch tape sides of cellophane together.

Present basket with front side facing the receiver.

How to Make a Bow

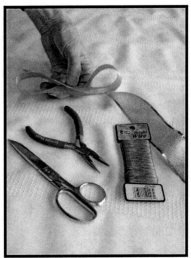

Select color-coordinated ribbon (wire edged is easiest to work with).

Make loops:

- Three loops on either side for small basket
- Five loops for medium size basket
- Seven loops for large basket

Twist one side of ribbon to keep patterned side out.

Add 8 inch straight piece of ribbon in the middle of the bow which will be used to secure bow to the basket.

Wrap wire around the loops and tail, twist the wire, then cut with wire cutters.

Cut tail ends into reverse 'V' shape.

Secure the bow to the cellophane at the top of the basket.

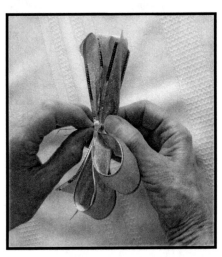

Selecting a Theme for the Basket

Cooking
Cooking magazine,
recipe—unusual
ingredients for recipe
Pot holder
Pan

Coffee/Tea
Fancy cup (take out of
box and set on top)
Coffee
Candy
Macadamia nuts (be
sure person is not
allergic and is able to
chew)
Cookies

Gardening
Gloves
Plant tags
Seeds—unusual
Gardening magazine
Trowel
Bulbs

Aroma Therapy
Candle holder, candle
Lotions
Soaps

Notes
Paper in different pretty
boxes
Note pads with similar
theme—kittens, dogs,
flowers, etc.
Pens

Food
Cookies (home-made or
purchased)
Pastry
Juice bottles or cans
Water bottles

Tools
New or old screw drivers
Pliers
Nails—small for pictures
Small saw
Needle nose screwdriver

Guidelines for Filling and Decorating Baskets

Obtain	Decorate	Fill	
Purchase new	Ribbons	Food Pictures	
Purchased at thrift store like Goodwill	Paper—colored cellophane	Music tapes Books	
	Cloth with color or design for theme	**Men**	**Women**
Homemade		Tools	Flowers
		Baseball	Fabrics
Old basket stored in attic or basement	Paper flowers	Golf ball Fish lures	Lavender sachet
	Name of homebound person	Trophy Rocks	Cards Knick knacks Lotion

Deliver	Enjoy	Share
In person	Visitor and visitee	Others living in facility
By mail		Staff coming into home
	Family of visitee	
Other person		Other visitors
	All week long	
Store		Grandchildren or family
	Until next visit	

Questions

1. Describe the most memorable basket you have received.

2. How did you feel about receiving the basket?

3. What would be a note of faith you or your visitee might put into a basket?

4. Do you think a care basket is only for a woman?

5. How might your visitee help create a care basket for someone special?

[1]Friesen, Delores, "Baskets of Faith," in *All Are Witnesses*, Kindred: Hillsboro, KS. 1996.

Chapter Six

Occupational Activities

Illustrations and Guidelines for Using Occupational Activities

Ted and Rives—Indoor gardening

On his second visit Ted found Rives quite disinterested in general conversation. Ted seemed to hit a blank wall in every conversational direction he tried. So he thought about some of the questions that were on the assessment sheet (See Appendix B) to refresh his memory about hobbies and things Rives liked to do.

He had noted gardening but Rives would be physically unable to do much gardening, even though it was a favorite hobby in past years. Since he had listened to Rives happily describe his previous farm work he brought up the

"Whatever you do, whether in word or deed, do it all in the name of the Lord Jesus, giving thanks to God the Father through Him."

Colossians 3:17

idea of setting up a mini flower garden near a window.

After discussing more plans with Rives about what he'd like to watch grow, Ted purchased a pottery planter, 14 inches in diameter with 4 inch high sides. Rives agreed to try growing a bonsai tree and a few orchids. He had a sunny window that seemed to provide good light.

On the next visit Ted brought garden supplies. "Rives, I'll put this planter on the table and you can add the dirt and use the shovel to transfer the plants to the pot." Ted moved a table, covered it with old newspapers, and put the garden things on the table so Rives could reach it.

For the next ten minutes Rives worked at assembling his garden. When he finished Ted went to the kitchen sink and brought a small watering can of water and opened the fertilizer bag. Rives stirred in the fertilizer and then carefully poured it around the plants.

"I really like my little garden. I can watch it every day and check it for moisture," Rives happily responded. "Before you know it, I'll be giving you an orchid for your wife," Rives called as Ted let himself out the door.

Rita and Susan—Reading

"Are you interested in talking a little more about the idea of reading something together? Remember, we discussed that Activity Assessment Sheet (See Appendix B) during our last visit?" Rita pulled her chair to the right side because she knew that Susan could hear better with her right ear.

"Yes, I would like to talk about it," Susan began, "but I could only bring my Bible when I moved here. I don't have any books around to read."

"I have some books at home, but you know we have books in our church library and then there is the public library where we can get books." Rita hoped that Susan would not be too concerned about how to get a book. "What kind of books are your favorites?"

"I always liked to read books about missionaries," Susan stated. "In Sunday school we often suggested books to the children that described missionary adventures."

"I like that kind too. Did you ever read *Through Gates of Splendor* by Elizabeth Elliott?" Rita asked.

"You know, I always wanted to. Back in the 70's a lot of people were talking about it. But somehow I just never got to it," Susan replied a bit sheepishly.

"I did read it, but it has been more than 30 years ago. I think another generation of folks is reading it now because of the new movie that describes how the missionaries were killed and what has happened since then," Rita explained. "I don't want to see the movie—I hear it is very tense in places. But I would like to read the book again."

"I would like to read the book. Now I have lots of time," Susan wistfully commented. "Do you think that we could get copies?"

"I'm sure that there is a copy in the library. One of my friends will have a copy if we can't get the library copy. Goodwill might also have old copies," Rita kept thinking of inexpensive book sources.

"I could pay for a copy," Susan volunteered. "There aren't many people here who read, but maybe somebody else could read it after I have finished with it."

"I'll check around to get copies for us," Rita said. "It would be good to talk about some of the people in the book. After I read it years ago, I heard someone suggest that there could have been a different ending. We might talk about that. But God has used the missionaries' deaths to bring more people to Christianity," Rita stopped to let Susan comment.

"I would not want to change God's plan, but I think that talking about the feelings the families had after the death of their husbands and fathers would be good. I don't think that I could forgive people for brutal murder," Susan admitted.

"I'll try to get books for us by next week," Rita assured Susan as she got ready to leave.

Liz and Adelle—Making a reminiscence box

Liz knew Adelle pretty well, so she didn't choose to actually complete the Activity Assessment (Appendix B). But in reviewing the hobbies Adelle enjoyed, Liz had an idea. She spent a few hours exploring the toy and craft shop and then stopped at a discount paper store. She was gathering a few things to put into a reminiscence box for Adelle. She recalled that Adelle had sent many cards to service people over the years, so she wanted to get some paper that they could use to write notes to people at church or elsewhere.

Adelle had also baked lots of cookies for Sunday School, Vacation Bible School and other church events. So Liz thought that a miniature mixing spoon or eggbeater, bowl and small plate from a toy store might jog Adelle's memory of a few of her previous activities. Liz secretly hoped that one day Adelle would even get interested in baking cookies in the kitchenette the care center maintained for residents use. Liz was trying to give Adelle something to do so that her sadness would not completely take over her life.

Before she went to visit Adelle, Liz dusted out an old shoebox that she had in her closet. She found some pretty paper and covered the box. She decorated the lid with a miniature set of measuring spoons labeled—pinch, dash, and smidgen—she'd received as a door prize once. She pasted a ribbon on the side of the box arranging it so that she could tie several ball point pens into it. Then she put the miniature kitchen tools and paper inside.

She was pleased with the shoebox and its contents that she carried into Adelle's room Thursday morning. Adelle was in her wheelchair with her back to the door—her usual spot. "Hi, Adelle," Liz called loudly enough to awaken Adelle, who seemed to always be asleep when she arrived. "I've brought something to show you today."

"Hello," Adelle responded a bit less than enthusiastic. "I was asleep." She looked sleepily at the box Liz placed in her lap.

"From some of the things we have talked about and what I remember of your activities I have made a 'Remember' box for you," Liz explained. "You can look at the things in it and think about how you used them and when I and others come you can tell us stories about using them. Your friends and family can bring little things to add to the box."

After Adelle looked at the contents, Liz asked, "What

else should I get to put inside?"

"I don't know, I never did much that could go in a box," Adelle mumbled.

"We can use miniature rather than real-life size things," Liz explained. "Several real size things, though, in this box are paper, envelopes and the pens that I tied on here, outside the box. I thought that we might write a letter together that you could send to someone," Rita accounted for some of the items in the box.

Hazel and Betty—Making a visitor book

"Did you have any visitors come to see you this week?" Hazel asked Betty.

"You are the only one who ever comes to see me. All I do is lie here all the time and hope that someone will come," Betty expressed her sense of being alone.

Hazel talked a little more with Betty and when she left she went to the nurses' station and asked if Hazel's family or other friends ever came to see her.

"Compared to other residents, Betty probably would hold the record for visitors. Her daughter was here shortly after breakfast. Another friend came shortly before lunch and her granddaughter stopped in to eat lunch with her. You came just after her nap and her son usually stops in on his way home from work," the desk clerk told Hazel.

Hazel realized that Betty probably forgot a lot of the events occurring in her day. Then she remembered that years ago she had a guest book that she invited guests to sign when they came to her home. That really helped her to remember who had been there. She decided that Betty needed a guest book too.

On her way home she stopped at a stationery store and found that the new guest books were very fancy and did not really have the right kinds of spaces for visitors to write much. So she chose some card stock for the cover, paper and ribbon. At home she made a sample page:

Date/time	Visitor's Name	Note of Conversation or Activity

Then she put in five lines and then repeated the heading. She was able to put records for six visits on a standard typing sheet of paper. Using the church copier she made 30 copies of the page, punched holes through the paper and the colored cardstock she chose for a cover. She tied ribbons through each hole and attached a pen so that visitors could sign the book whenever they came. She put a flower on the front of the book with an attractive note that read:

Please sign the book when you visit so that Betty and her family will know that you stopped in to see her. Betty sometimes has difficulty remembering that people visit her. Thank you for helping us know that you were here.

On her next visit, she showed Betty the book and explained that it was for visitors to write a note to her. Betty was very pleased and when the family saw Hazel at church the next Sunday, they expressed appreciation for making the book. They said that Betty did not remember very well and often told them that no one else had been there, but when they checked the book she had made they found that on most days at least three people visited Betty.

Connie and Bonnie—Setting up a bird feeder

Connie and Bonnie had been talking near the window while they both watched a sparrow and then a robin perch for a moment on the windowsill.

"Say, Bonnie, the birds like your window. What would you think about getting one of those cute little feeders and attaching it to your windowsill," Connie asked.

"Why, you know I'd never thought of that. A feeder would bring more birds and I could watch them. Since I can't hear well, I don't like to socialize too much with my neighbors," Bonnie stated. "Watching the birds would give me something to do."

They then spent time deciding what kind of feeder to get and Connie said she would check with the local stores to see what they had. Bonnie decided that she wanted one that she could fill with grain by just reaching out of her open window.

On her visit a week later Connie brought the bird feeder, and her husband, who was able to attach the bird feeder to the windowsill. It was on a pivoting extension so Bonnie could pull it close to her to fill and then turn it so that it extended from the window by 18 inches. They didn't want the birds to see their reflection in the glass and bang into Bonnie's window.

As she filled the feeder Bonnie smiled and then turned it away from the window. Bonnie and Connie and her husband were delighted when two sparrows almost immediately flew to the feeder and began pecking on the seeds.

Mary and June—Writing life stories

After Mary took a class on writing life stories, she told June about it. "I would like to write down some of the nursing stories you have told me."

"Oh my stories aren't anything," June seemed embarrassed about writing down any of her nursing experiences.

"Well, let's try and see how one comes out," Mary responded. "I will just ask you questions and you can answer them. I'll use my tape recorder to get all the details."

Guidelines for Writing Life Stories

Story-writing Oregon Resource Person—
   Betty Chapman Plude 503 838-4039

Trigger Words	Steps	Ways to Record	Use	Scripture Basis
Childhood play Life-changing experiences High School Favorite teacher Favorite pets Special comfort foods as a child or as an adult	1. Write down trigger words. 2. Write story based on trigger words. 3. Read story to person who told it—Give copy to family members or other groups that might value it. 4. Make a story album of treasured family memory.	Tape record Visitor takes notes Home-bound person writes	Local group Family Newspaper Coffee table album	Israelites built memorials of stones to mark special events— reminders to tell story to children. (Joshua 4:12) Moses recorded stories of Israelites. Jesus used stories to illustrate spiritual truths.

June's Story Written by Mary

It happened on a day when June had worked as night supervisor for 12 hours—from 7 p.m. to 7 a.m. It seemed to her as if she had just gotten to sleep when her sister, Maryann, called her. (She was living in her sister's upstairs bedroom for that year.)

"June, we need you! Julie (her four-year old daughter) just came in and looks awful," Maryann called upstairs where June was sleeping because she worked nights. June bolted out of bed hearing the anxiety in Maryann's voice. "What happened?" June was immediately alert.

"Julie spit out one of the pills that the neighbor man takes. The Smith children (next door neighbors) were playing doctor-nurse and making the little kids (their 'patients') take real pills. Anita gave pills to her younger sister Bernice (8), Tommy (5) and Julie, and tried to make the kids swallow them. Her brother and sister did, but Julie knew she wasn't supposed to take things like pills. With so much pressure she finally bit into it, but the taste was so bitter she ran home and spit it out on the porch."

June had no idea what the pills were that the children were playing with. One look at little Julie told her that she was pretty frightened. When June asked her to show her the pill, Julie led her to the corner of the porch where she spied a turquoise-colored capsule with a red circle around it that she immediately recognized as a sleeping pill. Knowing the neighbor man to be a 300 pound steeple-jack, she guessed this was a full strength sedative. It looked as if Julie had just bitten into it—the full capsule was there and lots of powder had tumbled out.

"How much did you swallow?" June asked.

"I didn't swallow any because it tasted so bad," Julie tearfully responded.

June directed her sister to have Julie wash her mouth

out with lots of water and told her that Julie should be fine—but she needed to watch her for any unusual drowsiness.

Hurrying over to the neighbor children, June found that the babysitter had fallen asleep and the 10-year-old had gotten into the medicine cabinet. The children were still in the yard playing with the bottles. She had been right—the label on the mostly empty bottle confirmed her initial judgment that the capsules were strong sedatives. She asked the children about how many they had taken. Tommy, the five-year-old, had swallowed two or maybe three. The other girl had only swallowed one.

June told the children that they were playing with dangerous pills. She quickly scooped up the pills and the bottle—gave them to the babysitter who had suddenly awakened and was very alarmed. She looked at Tommy and saw him beginning to fall asleep on the couch.

It was really hard for June to awaken him and make him walk around. She knew she had to do something because she was afraid that he would go into a sedative-induced coma. The parents weren't home so they couldn't take him to the hospital to have his stomach pumped. So June did the next best thing—she held him up making him walk around to prevent the sedatives from putting him into a coma.

When their mother returned an hour later June explained what had happened and told the mother that it would be best for her to give Tommy lots of fluids and make sure he stayed awake for the next few hours. When she called their doctor, Mrs. Smith said the doctor told her that June had saved her son's life. Without constant exercise and lots of fluids, his body would have absorbed the medication and he would be in a coma.

Returning home June checked her niece again and

found her just fine—busy playing with her dolls. Maryann thanked June for helping Julie and praised her for stepping in to help the neighbor children. By the time June got back to bed, she was too stimulated to sleep. But she wasn't about to take a sleeping pill!

At her next visit Mary gave June a copy of the story. June made a few corrections and they decided to send it to the local nursing school. They hoped the pediatric teacher might use it as an illustration.

Review at a Glance

Social Activities/Hobbies

Reading	Indoor Gardening	Reminiscence Boxes	Photo Album Organizing
Select reading by Interest/Concern	**Select type** Houseplants Herbs	**Type** Picture Miniature	**Collect** *(Family may help)*
Reading Taste Heroes Travel Novel Non-fiction	Flowers Vegetables Bonsai Force bulbs or branches	Music Poem **Questions** Where born?	Pictures, label them Cards Scenes
Identify top three Read sections Identify characters Identify actions Identify problems	Pussy willow Forsythia Flowering tree **Assemble equipment**	Family-farm or city? What kind of work did you do? Did you take trips? What kinds of	Equipment Scissors Album Special shape cutters
Consult librarian New books like favorites	Your garage Store **Plan garden**	hobbies? Stories about important life	Paper Glue sticks **Sort** Time
Read Individually Together aloud	Location Light Indoor/Outdoor Size	events **Develop themes that reflect**	Event Size Number
Activities Write letter to one of the characters Create different ending Draw scene described in book Talk about feelings	Layout **Discuss care** Water—who? Fertilizing Other **Plant** Follow package directions	**person's life** Activities Work Children Joys Hardships Other **Stimulate all senses** Crinkle of taffeta	**Themes** Childhood Work Hobbies School days **Resource person** Friend Scrapbook rep **Individual or together**
Adaptations for reading Large print materials Lighted magnifiers Books on tape Book holder	Consult other gardener resources Help person to do this if he/she can	Feel of marbles Smell cloves/perfume Sound of chalk Harmonica Taste of life saver	Decide who can do which activities Cut and paste

65

Review at a Glance

Occupational Activities/Hobbies

Phone Calling	Bird-Feeding	Table Games/Puzzles	Grooming
Cell phone Phone-book	**Select Feeder** Hanging on tree Mount on post Shape/size **Hang Feeder** Backyard Front yard Near window Window ledge **Fill Feeder** Arrange for person **Clean Feeder** Person Neighbor **Repair Feeder** Person Neighbor or visitor **Re-hang Feeder** Neighbor Staff Visitor **Use** Binoculars Bird book	**Select** Interest Ability Space **Source** Person Visitor Library Church Friends **Time** Energy available in day **Examples** Great North American Bird Watching Trivia Crossword Puzzles Hangman Mental Aerobics **Tips** Get easy to handle giant print (enlarge on copier) Make card holders Use non-slip paper	Manicure Set hair Help with make -up Find and put jewelry on Assist with shaving (electric razor)

Questions

1. Which of the occupational activities identified here have you and your visitee engaged in?

2. Are there any that you might try at an upcoming visit?

3. Could you and your visitee play table games or possibly enjoy pets together?

4. Have you ever written down some of the stories that your vistees tell you about their lives? (These might become a visitee's family treasures.)

5. Can your visitee write anything down, or possibly type on a computer?

6. Do you have ideas about other occupational activities you might do together?

Chapter Seven

Understanding Impaired Communication

Illustrations of Impaired Communications

Charlotte and Chris—Hearing Loss

Charlotte came home quite dissatisfied with the dynamics of her visit with Chris. Somehow she hadn't been able to get any decent conversation going. She felt like she'd been playing the old 'Telephone' party game. Only this time she was not at a party. She had just tried to talk with Chris, but she couldn't. Even her first words were misinterpreted. She recalled the beginning of their conversation:

"Hello Chris," Charlotte greeted Chris.

"A word aptly spoken is like apples of gold in settings of silver."

Proverbs 25:11

"The Sovereign Lord has given me an instructed tongue, to know the word that sustains the weary." Isaiah 50:4a

"No, it isn't <u>low</u> today," Chris had responded.

"I was just greeting you," Charlotte attempted to explain.

"I'm getting along well for my age," Chris noted.

And the whole 15 minutes had continued with similar confusions. Chris sometimes heard well, but put a different meaning to the words. Other times Charlotte had to repeat her question and wait an eternity for Chris to respond. She had tried to ask questions so that Chris would need to respond with several words, but usually Chris ignored those. When she repeated words Chris had just used, Chris just smiled at her.

Liz and Adelle—Speech difficulty

After Adelle's stroke Liz found that she needed to employ different skills to understand her. She began as usual.

"Hi Adelle, I've come for our visit."

"Ohhhhh you cccccame to see me?" Adelle became very excited.

"Take your time, you don't have to talk quickly," Liz reassured Adelle.

"Will you.....," Adelle stopped in tears.

"Are you trying to think of a word?" Liz asked. Adelle nodded.

"Let's see—just take a minute to think." Liz waited.

"Will you get my sweater? I'd like to go outside with you." Adelle smiled because she had been able to come up with the word "sweater".

"Sure, and I will even help you get your left arm in first

because it does not move as easily," Liz said as she went to the closet to get the sweater.

"Let's remember what your speech therapist told us," Liz reminded Adelle. "I need to take paper and pencil for you to <u>write</u> a word down in case you can't think how to speak it. I have all afternoon, so we are not rushed today."

Steve and Tom—Short Term Memory Loss

"Did you have a good breakfast," Steve asked Tom as he stopped by for a short visit.

"I guess so, I really can't remember what I had," Tom responded.

"Well you may have had toast and coffee like I did," Steve replied but then decided to change the conversation. Steve had forgotten that Tom was so forgetful. In years past he recalled that Tom had prided himself on remembering everything—phone numbers, addresses and even the license plate numbers of his friends' cars.

"Tell me, do you still recall the license plate of your 1960 Mustang?" he moved to a long term memory area so that Tom would not feel discouraged.

"I sure do. That little fire-engine red car was LWB 268," Tom was quick in reciting this.

Julia and Tina—Repetition of Questions

"Will you take me home now?" Tina asked when Julia visited her.

"This is your home," Julia explained for the fourth time in five minutes. "Tina, do you remember those white licorice-tasting cookies that you used to make at Christmas?" Julia asked, wanting to change the subject so the conversation would flow more easily.

"Do you mean *Springerle*? They were white, but they had anise flavoring, not licorice," Tina explained.

"Oh, I guess I forgot. I always liked to look at those cookies for awhile before taking a bite. They had such pretty designs," Julia added.

"Those cookies were made with a special rolling pin with the design in the wooden roller. When it was rolled over the dough the design imprint remained in the dough," Tina explained.

Julia found that when she talked about things that had occurred years ago, Tina became involved in the conversation and forgot about repeating her questions for a little while.

Guidelines for Impaired Communication

Repetition of questions:

- Try asking about something different to move away from the repetitive pattern.
- Find things in the environment to discuss, e.g. walk around the home or yard and have the person tell you about what you are seeing.
- Bring props along for show and tell, e.g. the church bulletin, an Ideals Magazine with religious poems and pictures, other magazine or book with scenic pictures, to help direct the conversation in different ways.

Short term memory loss:

- Avoid quizzing visitee, rather offer information instead, e.g. remind them of your name, let them know the current date and day of the week.
- Ask family to help put together an autobiographical memory book where the person can look up information, find pictures labeled with family members' names, etc.

Speech difficulty:

- Use yes or no questions as much as possible.
- Use body language and pantomime, especially if the person has difficulty understanding as well as speaking.
- Bring activities that don't require talking, e.g. music, a videotape of the worship service, a tea party.
- Stay relaxed and don't try too hard while listening—this decreases the stress to the person with the speech difficulty, and sometimes helps you understand. Give the person plenty of time to speak.
- If a person has *aphasia*, or difficulty articulating, the use of paper and pen or a wipe-off board may help.

Hearing loss:

- Get the person's attention before you start to speak.
- Make sure the lighting is good so visitee can see your face whenever you speak.
- Turn off any background noise and find a quiet place to visit.
- Find out if the person has a better ear and sit towards that side.
- Keep your hand away from your mouth and avoid chewing gum or doing anything else which makes it hard to watch your mouth while you are speaking.
- Be sure the person's hearing aid is in place if one is used. (You may need to ask a staff member or visitee to insert a new battery if visitee is unable to hear easily.)
- Bring a pad of paper and pen along just in case you can't get through by speech.

Deafness:

- If visitee uses a sign language interpreter, speak directly to visitee, not to the interpreter.
- If you bring a video or DVD along make sure it is captioned.

Visual loss:

- Always introduce yourself to visitee when you approach.
- Describe the surroundings and what is happening—paint a picture with words.

Mobility impairment:

- Sit at the visitee's level.
- Avoid touching the wheelchair—this is considered an extension of the visitee's body.

Review at a Glance

Understanding Communication in Specific Impairments

Mobility Impairment	Visual Loss	Auditory Loss	Speech Difficulty	Aphasia
Sit rather than stand or assume a position that puts you at eye level to your visitee with whom you want to communicate. This avoids muscle strain for your seated visitee attempting to look at you. Try to get into a position that is comfortable to you and allows your visitee to see your face without straining. Fatigue occurs quickly whenever the body is forced into awkward positions. If your visitee is in a wheelchair, it may be possible to move it so that the setting and position are more conducive to conversation.	Speak clearly to your visitee giving your name as you come into the room where your friend is located. Be sure that you don't speak louder unless your visitee is also hard of hearing as it is the first impulse to raise one's voice when conversation is difficult. Remember that a visitee with a visual impairment probably can't see non-verbal gestures, or at best may misinterpret them. Use a touch on the shoulder to get attention before speaking and be sure to indicate when you are leaving the room. Contact vendors to find sources of books and other materials on tape. Make any written notes in large print and provide large print materials if your visitee has some degree of sight.	Be sure your visitee can see your face when you are speaking at a distance between three and six feet away. If your visitee hears better in one ear, sit on that side, but do not speak directly into the ear as this usually distorts the sound. Get your visitee's attention before speaking using a touch on the arm if it is dark or nighttime. Speak slowly and distinctly in a well-modulated voice without high-pitched yelling. It may help (if you are female) to wear a clearly visible lipstick that outlines your lips. Emphasize words with exaggerated facial movements, and body language. Write down important information. Turn lights on when speaking.	Sit or take a position so that you directly face your visitee. Ask your visitee to speak very slowly. Practice good listening skills to become familiar with your visitee's voice inflections and other characteristic sounds or movements that represent particular thoughts or words. Keep paper and pencil handy or some other letter board so your visitee can write or form words using these aids. Plan longer visits because visiting may require repetition and consequently more time. Don't constantly try to fill in words and second-guess what your visitee is trying to say. Don't continue to the point of frustration, for your visitee or yourself, trying to understand words that are unclear.	*(Advanced Speech Difficulty)* Allow adequate time for the visitee to form words. Ask questions that can be answered with a head nod. Use various visual movements to help clarify your own or visitee's words Bring any kinds of visuals such as a flash card or word board along, or use those to which your visitee usually has access. Speak of things familiar and of interest to visitee. Talk as if the visitee understands, avoiding childish words.

Questions

1. What is a key point to consider when talking with visitees who have the following deficits?

    Mobility impairment

    Visual loss

    Auditory loss

    Speech difficulty

    Aphasia

2. What kinds of abnormal speaking patterns have some of your visitees had?

3. Which of the pointers about talking to people who have communication deficits have you found useful?

4. Have you had any other talking or communicating difficulties on your visits?

5. What other approaches have you used to help conversation when you encountered communication difficulties?

Chapter Eight

Nutritional Concerns

Illustrations of Key Nutritional Concerns

Kelli and Miranda—Ethnic food treats

"Oh, I'd love some *apfel moos*," Miranda exclaimed to her visitor. "It seems as if it has been years since I've had some. Mother made it when I was a kid. And when the summer apples were ripe I always made some too."

"Miranda, if you tell me how to cook it, I'd be happy to prepare some for you," Kelli volunteered.

"Would you?" Miranda's eyes lit up. "It's not hard. You just peel two apples, slice them, and cook them with half a cup of water until they are soft. Then mix one-third cup of sugar and two tablespoons of flour together well. Add two cups of milk to the flour and sugar stirring until it's smooth.

"That everyone may eat and drink, and find satisfaction in all his toil—This is the gift of God."

Ecclesiastes 3:13

While you are stirring the apples, gradually add the sugar and flour mixture to the apples and boil until thick. It may curdle, but just keep on stirring and it will be okay."

"I think I could do that. It's really like apple pudding, isn't it?" Kelli was satisfied that she had the idea. "I'll bring you some when I come to visit next time," Kelli promised.

Bill and Henry—Diabetes

Before he went to visit Henry, Bill decided to pick up a candy bar—one with that heart-healthy dark chocolate he'd been reading about.

As he walked in, Bill handed the candy treat to Henry.

"Oh," Henry sighed and didn't reach out eagerly for the candy bar. "I'm diabetic. My blood sugar was high this morning, so I'd better not, even though I love those Mound bars. I have to watch my carbs."

"I'm sorry, I didn't think about that," Bill apologized and felt like kicking himself for his forgetfulness. "Are there any things that you can eat that would be a treat for you?"

"Maybe one day you could bring me some plain popcorn—without salt or butter," Henry responded making a wry face. "I'd like good old caramel corn, but it's out. Plain popcorn would give me the idea as it touches my tongue."

Mary, Ted and Ken—Liquid caution

Mary and Ted walked in to visit Ken. Ken had just moved from his home of 35 years to the care center. Consequently everything was new for him.

"Hi Ken!" Ted greeted him as he extended his hand. Ken shook his hand warmly and then asked Ted if he would get him a cup of coffee. Ted went to the nursing station to ask for coffee. When the assistant learned it was for Ken she said, "I'll fix the coffee for him. He chokes on straight liquid so we add a thickener to it."

When Ted handed the coffee to Ken he took a quick look at it and sighed, "I'd hoped you would bring me a regular cup. I don't much like it thick."

"The nurse said that you needed to have it thickened to keep from choking," Ted explained.

"They say so. But my stroke affected my arm, not my throat," Ken snorted.

On returning home Ted decided to check the internet and found out that with a stroke one side of the throat can also be affected because of the location of the blood clot in the brain affecting all the nerves on the affected side. Then Ted understood why Ken might have trouble swallowing on one side. He wouldn't have enough motor function to swallow because of the nerve paralysis. Ted fervently hoped and prayed that Ken could soon get his swallowing ability back. He decided he agreed with Ken, thickened coffee somehow just isn't right for anyone to have to slurp for long.

Sue and Ellen—Food allergies

Sue stopped at her favorite pie shop for two pieces of their specialty—lemon meringue, to take as a treat for Ellen.

When she walked in to Ellen's room, she told Ellen she'd brought a treat. But when she showed Ellen the pieces of pie Ellen's face fell.

"Oh, don't you like lemon meringue?" Sue asked.

"Yes, I do—I love it," Sue replied wistfully. "But I have a

gluten allergy and I can't eat pie crust."

"Oh never mind about the crust. I often leave it anyway," Sue confessed.

"I'd like to eat the lemon filling, but I don't know what they use to thicken it. Maybe we could call the pie shop and find out if they used cornstarch or wheat flour. If they used corn starch I can eat it, but if the lemon pudding has a wheat-based thickener, I'd have a severe problem with diarrhea and gas."

Sue immediately called the shop and learned that they used only corn starch as a thickener. So they both enjoyed the lemon custard and the meringue, but left the crust for different reasons—Ellen because of allergy and Sue because of calories.

Guidelines for Bringing Food

- Some foods are considered **comfort** foods—chicken soup, potato soup, chicken and dumplings, homemade spaghetti. **Special Note**: When bringing in soups and other dishes, be sure to bring a portion visitees likely can consume at a meal. Too much is overwhelming and may turn off their appetite.

- Older visitees with poor appetites need high calorie foods like milkshakes or custards made with whole milk.

- In season, bring foods from your garden, or from the local market because fresh foods contain more nutrients -- more vitamins and minerals.

- Bring freshly baked items. If possible bring a small amount of bread, muffin or cookie dough ready to bake and put it into the oven at the visitee's home. The aroma of fresh baking stimulates the appetite.

• Visitees who have dentures or dental problems may need soft foods to make chewing easier.

• Bring foods with protein or other healthy nutrients rather than primarily sweet desserts.

• Bring foods in disposable containers or transfer food to visitee's dishes to avoid the extra work of returning the pots and dishes.

• When possible eat treat with visitee. Eating together creates a special kind of bonding.

• Talking with visitee or caregiver before bringing food items helps avoid allergy, food dislikes and other eating problems.

• Be cautious about bringing foods commonly causing allergies such as peanuts, soy, shell fish, eggs, and milk/dairy.

• Visitors need to ask visitees about allergies and food preferences prior to bringing food to visitees.

Review at a Glance

Food Treats

Food Treats	Sanitary	Sugar/ Diabetes	Vegetarian	Special Diets	Ethnic Foods
Something not usually eaten—not daily fare. Garden foods. Special foods like spaghetti or home-made bread.	Cleanliness in food preparation is essential.	Sugar adds calories-limited for those overweight. Diabetes —Foods with sugar and high carbs must be carefully monitored and balanced throughout the day.	No meat. Eggs and milk may also be omitted.	No liquid for persons with stroke because they may choke with muscles paralyzed. Low salt for certain kidney and blood pressure problems. Soft food for those without teeth. Check for food allergies.	*Apfel Moos* Egg Roll Tacos Pizza Chicken Soup

Questions

1. What kind of special food treats have you brought to your visitees?

2. What would be a comfort food for you?

3. What kinds of foods have your visitees said are their comfort foods?

4. Do you know about any special dietary needs your visitees have? Do any have dentures?

5. What other tips have you found to be useful when bringing food to visitees?

Chapter Nine

Death of Visitee and Visitor Coping

Illustrations and Guidelines Related to Visiting the Dying

Ted and Rives—Life Review

"Hi Ted, just thought I'd give you a call to let you know that Dad has changed a bit," Richard, Rives' son paused.

"Is he weaker and sicker—having more pain?" Ted asked.

"Well, I haven't noticed any big changes. Dad has had so much pain for so long that it's hard to tell," Richard responded. "But I find that he's more withdrawn and quieter than usual."

"Do you think he's getting closer to death?" Ted

"When the perishable has been clothed with the imperishable, and the mortal with immortality, then the saying that is written will come true: 'Death has been swallowed up in victory'."

1 Corinthians 15:54

decided to find out if Richard was prepared for this. "I've read that some people become quieter and focus more internally as they anticipate death."

"It could be," Richard reflected. "He's never said that he wanted to die, but he knows his life has had drastic changes that keep him from walking around. Even though we know he isn't well, we haven't actually thought about losing Dad."

When Ted hung up, he wondered if he had interpreted the changes in Rives accurately. He hoped he hadn't alarmed Richard unduly.

The next morning Ted walked into Rives' living room. "Good morning Rives! How are the plants doing?" Rives was seated as usual—in his recliner chair that was raised up on blocks.

"They're not too good. I've forgotten to water them for a couple of days," Rives lamented.

"Well, I can water them for you this morning if you'd like," Ted said and started to go after the watering can.

"Yes, that would be good," Rives agreed and continued, "I'm just not good for much of anything anymore."

Ted watered the orchid plant and the miniature jade. When he finished he sat down beside Rives.

"I just hurt all over. Any kind of movement gives me terrible pain," Rives grimaced as he spoke.

"Maybe you should ask your doctor about some different pain pills," Ted suggested.

"I could, but I doubt they'd really help much. There comes a time....," and his voice trailed off.

Ted noticed that Rives almost seemed to be asleep. When he roused he resumed speaking, "I've had a good life. My wife and I moved as I changed jobs." He continued slowly recounting other significant events in his life.

When Rives paused, Ted looked at his watch and saw that he'd been there over an hour. He quickly left, afraid that so much talking would have tired Rives. Though Richard had said Rives was quieter, Ted found that Rives had talked on and on. Only, this was a different kind of talk. Rives had described his most significant life experiences.

Ted decided to call his pastor and ask to talk about what to do when visitees began reviewing key details of their lives. Pastor Clyde expressed appreciation for Ted's call. He explained that he had listened as other people did this. In doing some research, he told Ted that he had learned that this is common when people are conscious as they near death.

"As people approach death they frequently engage in a life review. It seems to be important to them to go over key events to put them into perspective. Listening to this review helps to understand the person a little better— hearing the experiences that were important to them during their lives. If there is any opportunity for the visitor to comment, it is good to offer hope. Sharing of stories that provide hope or reviewing meaningful life experiences is helpful. Of course there is heavenly hope, but even commenting positively on the life events the visitee shares will help focus on happy memories."

Ted and Rives—Desiring Heaven

"Has Rives expressed a desire to be in heaven with the Lord?" Pastor Clyde asked.

"Not exactly, but on my visit a week ago he mentioned how good it would be to see his parents again," Ted recalled.

"As persons near death they may talk about desiring death, to be in heaven with others and the Lord. They may express a keen longing to see their spouse, other family members and dear friends who have died. Some express a desire to have their spouse greet them and lead them to the Lord," Pastor Clyde spoke from his previous visits with persons nearing death.

"What can I say when he says he wants to go to heaven?" Ted expressed his own uncertainty with this direction in conversation.

"It is good if the person nearing death faces this with a positive outlook. The anticipation of being whole in body again, without physical problems such as difficulty hearing, seeing and moving is wonderful. Since Rives has had so much pain and suffering you might want to focus his thinking on release from this," Pastor Clyde added so that Ted had another cue for directing conversation.

"When some of these conversational changes occur, it is important to make every day a highlight. Planning small surprises, visits from friends, special foods, games, or conversation may be appreciated. Even if Rives can't participate much, just watching and observing some favorite pastimes may provide him a little pleasure." Pastor Clyde tried to give Ted some things to do so he did not feel at a loss.

Ken and Bill—Eternal Life

"Hi Bill." Ken greeted Bill as he had been for the ten months he visited with him. "How are you doing?"

"It isn't a very good day for me. I've been sick so long," Bill responded. "I have had so much pain in my legs and back. God doesn't hear my prayer anymore. In fact, I wonder if all this 'God' talk means anything. I think that I've lost my faith."

"Your faith has surely been tried. You have been through a lot." Ken was at a loss and didn't know what to say. He silently prayed for encouragement for Bill and left as soon as he could.

As he closed his car door, Ken grabbed his cell phone and called Pastor Clyde. "Pastor, I don't know what to say to Bill. He's losing his faith!"

"Oh Ken, that is hard. When do you plan to visit him next?" Pastor Clyde asked.

"I almost ran out of our visit today because I was so shocked by his comments. I was caught off-guard," Ken confided.

"Could you plan to visit him again tomorrow afternoon? I will go with you. We need to try to help Bill. I am sure that you were surprised because Bill has been such a pillar of faith and service in our church—a deacon and leader of Bible studies. I've found that Satan often attacks mature saints hard in moments of their physical weakness. I know that both you and I have prayed with Bill for his healing, but God has not chosen to heal him."

"I'm on vacation this week, so I can go to visit him tomorrow again, say about two o'clock?" Ken replied, glad not to make this visit alone.

Bill didn't even try to be cordial when Pastor Clyde and Ken arrived the next afternoon. He went right to his fear.

"I don't believe I have eternal life. I expect to die soon and get out of all this pain."

"Bill, you have struggled so many years and this last year has been so difficult. We want to share a few scriptures with you regarding our eternal life. I know that you have read 1 John 5:11-13 before. See, it says in verses 11 and 12 that God has given us eternal life in His Son. Verse 13 says that those who believe in the Son of God may know that they have eternal life. I think it was about 10 years ago when I heard you tell a new friend that you had eternal life because you believed that Jesus died for your sins." Pastor Clyde paused to give Bill a chance to respond.

"That was years ago. This is now and I just don't have that same belief anymore. Too much pain has been my lot," Bill grimaced as he spoke.

"God has chosen to make known that Christ is in us— according to Colossians 1:27. Just because you are feeling terrible does not change the fact that Christ is in you," Pastor Clyde stated emphatically.

"I sure don't sense His presence in all this pain," Bill reflected.

"It says in Hebrews 6:19 that we have hope as an anchor for our soul that is firm and secure. The next verse explains that Christ went before us and is now our High Priest forever—atoning for our sins," Pastor Clyde chose verses carefully.

"Guess I do need an anchor. My mind really takes off when the pain constantly hits me," Bill confessed.

"I want to share one more portion of scripture with you. Second Corinthians 5:1 states that God is building us an eternal house in heaven, one that is not made by human hands. Verse 2 states that 'Meanwhile we groan, longing to be clothed with our heavenly dwelling....' You are doing some literal groaning now in your pain. Verse 5 says that God has given us His Spirit as a guarantee for what is to come. Verse 7 is encouraging, 'We live by faith, not by sight.' I know that you would prefer to be away from your pain-wracked body and at home with the Lord as it says in verse 8. So Ken and I are going to pray that you experience a real sense of God's Spirit on your body and that God will take you to heaven to be with Him when He decides it is time." Pastor Clyde stopped. "Ken, will you pray for Bill now?"

"Dear God—Bill is in a lot of pain and this sometimes mixes up his thinking. I ask that Your Holy Spirit will give him the sense that because he believes in You he has eternal life. May he live by this faith, even though he does not see it fulfilled yet. Amen."

Before Pastor Clyde and Ken left, Bill thanked them for coming, adding that he did feel encouraged.

As they were driving back to church Ken expressed his heartfelt gratitude. "I really appreciate having you come with me on this visit. I didn't know how to help Bill with his concern about eternal life."

Linda and Leanne—Hard Questions

Linda found that Leanne, her visitee, asked many questions about heaven that were difficult to answer. So she decided to write the questions down:

1. What is heaven like?
2. Will I recognize people?
3. Will my friend who chose physician assisted death be in heaven?
4. What is the "Paradise" that Jesus referred to on the cross going to be like?
5. When do we go to the real heaven?
6. How do I know that I will go to heaven?

Linda then told Leanne that since she did not have all the answers, she would give the questions to their pastor and ask him to come with her for a visit and they could discuss answers to some of the questions. When Pastor Clyde and Linda visited Leanne he gave scripturally based responses to most of the questions.

What is heaven like?

"Well, Jesus said He is going to prepare a place for us. Some of the description in Revelation 21: 9-21 helps us understand it as indescribably beautiful. It shines with God's glory, with walls of jasper and the city is made of pure glass gold with the foundation of the city walls decorated with every kind of precious stone."

"I can't even imagine that kind of beauty," Leanne exclaimed.

Will I recognize people?

"There are scriptures that speak of introductions of people in white robes. I think that the Lord will be gracious in allowing us to recognize each other."

Will my friend who chose physician-assisted death be in heaven?

"I don't know, Leanne, but my thought is that it will depend on whether your friend ever accepted Jesus as personal Lord and Savior." Pastor Clyde tried to be as candid as he could be.

"If taking one's life is a sin, I hope that does not keep my friend out of heaven," Leanne commented wistfully.

What is the 'Paradise' that Jesus referred to on the cross going to be like?

"We don't have much biblical description of paradise except that we know that Jesus will be there." Pastor Clyde did not want to go beyond scripturally based instruction.

When do we go to the real heaven?

"This is another question that scripture does not expand on. I don't want to put a lot of ideas out there. The one thing that I am sure about is that it will be when God plans the time."

How do I know that I will go to heaven?

"The Bible says that we need to believe in Jesus and we will be saved. (Acts 16:31) Anyone who believes that Jesus died on the cross for his/her sins and asks for forgiveness of those sins will go to heaven," Pastor Clyde provided the basis of salvation.

"I do believe in Jesus, and I have asked Him to forgive me for my sins—so I will go to heaven when I die," Leanne smiled, expressing confidence in her salvation and her destination of heaven.

"I can rejoice with you, Leanne, that you are a Christian. The complete answers to some of your questions will have to wait until you and I are in heaven. But maybe the questions will be gone because we will <u>know</u> the answers when our spirits and minds become eternal."

Julia and Frances—Dealing with Death of Visitee

Julia visited Frances for almost a year. During that time they had become great friends. She learned a great deal about Frances. For example, Frances' husband died ten years before she moved to the care facility. They had no children and many of her friends had either died or become too feeble to visit her. On every visit Julia could see that Frances was becoming weaker. She could not take the 40 minute wheelchair ride anymore. She did not smile or talk as much. She expressed less interest in events around her and focused more internally on her own feelings and needs. Julia knew these were signs that indicated decreasing vitality, eventually leading to death.

On realizing this, Julia decided not to visit as much, trying to adjust to her own anticipated loss. But after she had skipped a week, Julia was sorry because Frances had missed her visit. "I didn't know where you were. I missed our tea-time chat so much." So then Julia added an extra visit each week. But somehow that wasn't quite right either. With the visits too close together there was not enough time to adequately prepare for the weekly visit to make it special. When Frances died, Julia struggled with her loss.

Julia wrote a letter to Pastor Clyde:

> "I find it hard to cope with some of the things that previously had been important, but now seem so shallow. I had to excuse myself from lunchroom conversations about the best place to get cheesecake. My learning to cope with loss was too fresh to become involved with such mundane things. When I look at pictures of Frances, they only bring fresh waves of loss. The picture doesn't talk and laugh with me as the real Frances did so often."

General Guidelines for Visiting Dying People

Pastor Clyde identified some guidelines for visitors in dealing with the visitees who are nearing death. He also suggested things homebound visitors might do to help themselves prepare for the loss of their visitee.

Suggestions for Visitors Who Encounter People Nearing Death

Be quiet and listen when in the presence of a dying person. Recognize this is a time of being on hallowed ground. Filler comments such as "You'll be in a better place" satisfy the visitor, but may be meaningless chatter to the one dying. When Jesus took Peter, James and John to the Mount of Transfiguration, Peter began talking of memorials (Mark 9:2-8) Peter was admonished to listen to the Lord and absorb the holy moment. Similarly in the holy presence of death, we usually need to be silent in waiting expectation.

Express emotion sensitively. When Jesus was with Mary and Martha following the death of Lazarus, He was deeply moved and He wept. (John 11:33-35) Following Jesus' model, we need to sensitively express our own emotions of grief and loss as the death of the person we're visiting approaches.

Express joy for/with the person who is going into the presence of the Lord when this might be helpful. Jesus said that if we love Him, we would rejoice because He is going to the Father. (John 14:28) At a moment when the visitee is thinking and speaking about dying, mentioning Jesus' statement about rejoicing in anticipation may change a potentially sorrowful moment to one of gladness.

Ways for Visitors to Develop Comfort with Death

- Spend time with the Lord. Pray about the experience of death and meditate on verses dealing with death. (References are easily identified using a Bible concordance.)

- Focus on heaven rather than on death. The expectation of being in heaven with the Lord transforms the finality of death as an end into a glorious hope and expectation.

- Consider the joy of eternally living with the Lord, rather than death ending life. The Christian anticipates eternal life in heaven.

- Spend time with Christians anticipating death who are rejoicing to go to be with the Lord. The Christian view of death removes the sorrow of loss and adds living forever in the presence of the One who gives us life now and eternally.

Suggestions for visitors in coping with grief and loss:

- Pray when you are ready—tell God about your pain and ask for His help--God's Spirit will lead you in this.

- Take walks or do some form of daily exercise.

- Begin a new hobby, if at all feasible, to absorb some time and energy.

- Read a book or watch a DVD related to death and dying or heaven.

- Write down painful thoughts that come to mind related to your loss of the person.

- Allow yourself plenty of time to readjust.

Review at a Glance: Death and Visitor Coping

	Visitee Concerns	Visitor's Responses		
Focus Points	Description	Ways to Respond	General Response Categories	Ways to Cope
Thoughts	Anger toward people and God. Personal regret. Personal anticipation of heaven.	Listen to anger and regrets. Talk about heaven as a real place.	Thinking about redirection.	Refocus sense of personal loss to thinking about the person pain-free and whole in body in the presence of the Lord.
Conversation	Life review. Topic of heaven. Regrets and disappointments.	Allow person to speak freely without censoring comments. Encourage hopefulness whenever this is realistic.	Helpful actions.	Walk Read Develop new hobby Journal Sing
Referrals	Spiritual needs Financial needs Physical needs	Refer to Pastor. Refer to group facilitator. Refer to parish nurse.	Identify people and resources for support for these needs.	Talk with friend who has lost a personal friend sometime earlier. Discuss with other visitors how they have coped.
Assurance of Eternal Life	Asks questions about being sure there is a God and whether the person is worthy and merits entrance into heaven.	Ask visitees what they base their faith on— Look for response indicating belief in Christ's atonement for personal sin – Romans 5:8 I John 5:11-13 Referral to Pastor	Scriptures to encourage. (Refer to topical references in Appendix A: Salvation).	Hebrews 6:10— God's blessing. II Cor. 1:3-4— God's personal comfort so that this can be passed on to others.
Prayer	Person begs to be allowed to die. Person begs for healing. Person pleads for comfort and greater measure of faith.	Pray for person in accord with requests— while present and in private prayer asking that God's will be done.	Prayer of thanks and gratefulness.	When able— Thank God for allowing you to meet and minister to such a special one of His saints.

Questions

1. What questions have you had from your visitors on the subject of heaven and dying?

2. How did you respond to these questions?

3. Which of Pastor Clyde's suggestions will be most helpful to you?

4. What is a good way to regroup following the death of your visitee?

Final Thoughts

If you have finished reading this handbook, now what? What should you do next? Here are two suggestions.

1. Form a discussion group

If you have not already participated in a group discussion of the material in this handbook, now would be a good time to establish a discussion group. Learning is always greatly improved when we study in a group. The book of Proverbs reminds us that "As iron sharpens iron, so one person sharpens another" (27:17) and that "Victory is won through many advisers" (11:14).

Following are some suggestions for projects which the group might do together to enhance learning:

- **Humor** Make scrapbooks of cartoons or humorous anecdotes that might be used on a visit.

- **Observation** Play a video of a real or staged visit and talk about observations that could be made.

- **Music** Set up a mini music library with portable DVD players that might be taken along on a visit.

- **Encouragement** Draw discouraged and encouraged facial sketches as a means of stimulating discussion about what people find to be encouraging.

- **Baskets** Put together baskets around a theme such as tea time or a holiday such as Valentine's Day.

- **Occupational Activities** Create a reminiscence box for your own life or for the life on someone you have visited.

- **Impaired Communication** Set up some role play situations to help you understand how to talk with someone who is hearing impaired, sight impaired, or wheelchair bound.

- **Nutrition** Bring samples of sugar-free foods, thickened coffee, and foods for other special diets (such as gluten -free foods).

- **Death** Bring in a resource person to talk about helping someone prepare for death.

2. Start making visits

Don't let this book lie on a shelf gathering dust! Reading alone will do no good unless the lessons learned are put into practice. It is the prayer of the author and those involved with publishing this material that readers will use the suggestions in this handbook to make visits to the homebound and hospitalized people—and to make those visits special occasions for all involved.

Appendix A

Alphabetical Listing of Scriptures and Prayers

Some lines are left blank so you can fill in the name of your visitee, or other detail that fits your visitee's situation.

Anger

Anecdote

"I hate you!" Bill shouted at his caregiver as Todd, his church visitor, stepped into the room.

"You must be very upset," Todd commented, wondering what to do. "Shall I come back another time?"

"No, he was just leaving," Bill replied nodding at his caregiver to leave. "I am sorry that you heard me scream like that. I just get so upset from my pain and the constant irritation of getting me to turn or transferring to a chair."

"I am sure that you do cope with a lot of pain," Todd responded. "Would it help if we talked about it? I even have some scriptures on anger that we could talk about. It is pretty hard to deal with all of the pain you have and the changes this brings to your life."

"I've never been an easy-going man and with this illness it seems that more of my feelings and anger come out than ever before. I become so upset I just can't hold it in. You know, I would like to go over some Bible verses about my anger."

As he spoke, Bill seemed to calm down.

Scriptures

"They refused to listen and failed to remember the miracles you performed among them. They became stiff-necked and in their rebellion appointed a leader in order to return to their slavery. But you are a forgiving God, gracious and compassionate, slow to anger and abounding in love." Nehemiah 9:17

"Refrain from anger and turn from wrath; do not fret—it leads only to evil." Psalm 37:8

"Yet he was merciful; he forgave their iniquities and did not destroy them. Time after time he restrained his anger and did not stir up his full wrath." Psalm 78:38

"The Lord is compassionate and gracious, slow to anger, abounding in love." Psalm 103:8

"A gentle answer turns away wrath, but a harsh word stirs up anger." Proverbs 15:1

"A hot-tempered man stirs up dissension, but a patient man calms a quarrel." Proverbs 15:18

"Better a patient man than a warrior, a man who controls his temper than one who takes a city." Proverbs 16:32

"Do not be quickly provoked in your spirit, for anger resides in the lap of fools." Ecclesiastes 7:9

"In your anger do not sin; Do not let the sun go down while you are still angry." Ephesians 4:26

"Get rid of all bitterness, rage and anger, brawling and slander, along with every form of malice." Ephesians 4:31

Prayer

God, please help me exchange my anger for Your love. Please give me the strength to control my temper. Lord, may I respond gently—not making_____ even more angry and upset by my words.

101

Death

Anecdote

"The doctor tells me there's nothing left to do. They can't treat me anymore." Don noted in a matter-of-fact manner.

"What is on your mind right now?" Jim wondered what Don must be thinking about this.

"I guess I'm not afraid of death. I believe in God and have confessed my sin, so I know that I will go to heaven, but I am not sure how painful it will be to die. I have to admit that death is a big unknown for me," Don paused to catch his breath and sort out his thoughts.

Scriptures

"The waves of death swirled about me; the torrents of destruction overwhelmed me. The cords of the grave coiled around me; the snares of death confronted me. In my distress I called to the Lord: I called out to my God. From his temple he heard my voice and my cry came to his ears." 2 Samuel 22:5-7

"...to those who long for death that does not come, who search for it more than for hidden treasure, who are filled with gladness and rejoice when they reach the grave? Why is life given to a man whose way is hidden, whom God has hedged in? For sighing comes to me instead of food; my groans pour out like water. What I feared has come upon me; what I dreaded has happened to me. I have no peace, no quietness; I have no rest, but only turmoil." Job 3:21-26

"Even though I walk through the valley of the shadow of death, I will fear no evil, for you are with me; your rod and your staff, they comfort me." Psalm 23:4

"For this God is our God for ever and ever; he will be our guide even to the end." Psalm 48:14

"My heart is in anguish within me; the terrors of death assail me. Fear and trembling have beset me; horror has overwhelmed me. I said 'Oh, that I had the wings of a dove! I would fly away and be at rest—I would flee far away and stay in the desert; I would hurry to my place of shelter, far from the tempest and storm'." Psalm 55:4-8

"For you [God] have delivered me from death and my feet from stumbling, that I may walk before God in the light of life. Psalm 56:13

"For you, O Lord, have delivered my soul from death, my eyes from tears, my feet from stumbling....Precious in the sight of the Lord is the death of his saints." Psalm 116:8, 15

"When calamity comes, the wicked are brought down, but even in death the righteous have a refuge." Proverbs 14:32

"There is a time for everything, and a season for every activity under heaven: a time to be born and a time to die,..." Ecclesiastes 3:1-2

"When you pass through the waters, I will be with you; and when you pass through the rivers, they will not sweep over you. When you walk through the fire, you will not be burned; the flames will not set you ablaze." Isaiah 43:2

"For I am convinced that neither death nor life, neither angels nor demons, neither the present nor the future, nor any powers, neither height nor depth, nor anything else in all creation, will be able to separate us from the love of God that is in Christ Jesus our Lord." Romans 8:38-39

"For as in Adam all die, so in Christ all will be made alive....When the perishable has been clothed with the imperishable, and the mortal with immortality, then the saying that is written will come true: 'Death has been swallowed up in victory. Where, O death, is your victory? Where O death, is your sting?' The sting of death is sin, and the power of sin is the law. But thanks be to God! He gives us the victory through our Lord Jesus Christ." 1 Corinthians 15:22, 54-56

Prayer

God _____ (Name) is ill and the human treatments are no longer effective. This is a hard time for him and his family. We ask that You will give _____ (Name) wisdom during this difficult time. Lord, he needs wisdom to make choices for himself and his family.

Please give him Your peace as he continues this journey. First, we pray for Your healing miracle to restore his health to overcome _____ (disease or problem). If You choose not to give health, we ask that You will supply Your comfort, Your peace.

Please help him to model Your love and grace even while his physical body is failing.

I pray for _____ (Names of family members) as they stand beside ____ (Name) in this trying hour.

We are grateful for Your comfort and love that You promise us. Amen

Fear

Anecdote

"Sally, I know I should not be afraid to have this surgery. I know the doctor is good. But I still feel fearful. What if they find an inoperable tumor?"

"Mrs. Brown, most people are fearful of surgery. So much is at stake. There are some Bible verses that have helped others—Let's read them together while I'm here and I'll write down the references so you can look them up yourself whenever you feel uneasy as you think about surgery."

Scripture

"Be strong and courageous. Do not be afraid or terrified because of them, for the Lord your God goes with you; he will never leave you nor forsake you." Deuteronomy 31:6

"When I am afraid, I will trust in you. In God, whose work I praise, in God I trust; I will not be afraid. What can mortal man do to me?" Psalm 56:3-4

"He who dwells in the shelter of the Most High will rest in the shadow of the almighty…. You will not fear the terror of night, nor the arrow that flies by day, nor the pestilence that stalks in the darkness, nor the plague that destroys at midday….If you make the Most High your dwelling—even the Lord, who is my refuge-" Psalm 91: 1, 5, 6, 9

Prayer

God, we thank you for your promise to be with us—to be our shelter and to give us rest from the fears that surface in our lone night time thoughts when sleep evades us. You also quiet our fears that arise from the events of the day.

You say we should be strong and courageous, but sometimes our fears overwhelm us. (May list specific things like surgery that visitee has noted.)

We are encouraged to trust you like David did when he was in mortal danger. You are the God who always is our refuge. You promise to always be with us. (May list some specific place visitee must go that evokes fear).

Because you are our God we can overcome our fear by trusting your faithfulness and loving care for saints in times past and for us now. We know that you are all-powerful even in this _____circumstance.

I pray that you will help _____ to be less afraid of his/her _____tomorrow. May s/he feel confident that You are guiding the doctors and nurses as they care for her/him.

Thank you that you always hear our prayers. Amen.

Healing

Anecdote

"I have so much pain. Sometimes I wonder why God allows me to live. He has heard me pray so often," Tom stopped and grimaced as he tried to move.

"Is your pain in your back?" Harry asked.

"It starts there and radiates down my leg. I can't take any steps now. It even hurts when I just lie in bed," Tom groaned audibly.

"Tom, you know we believe that God is our Great Physician. Here are a couple of verses on healing that you might find helpful. I'll read a few and write out the references for you so you can return to them later," Harry said reaching for his handbook.

Scriptures

"'If you listen carefully to the voice of the Lord your God and do what is right in his eyes, if you pay attention to his commands and keep all his decrees, I will not bring on you any of the diseases I brought on the Egyptians, for I am the Lord, who heals you'." Exodus 15:26

"'Go back and tell Hezekiah, the leader of my people, 'This is what the Lord, the God of your father David says: I have heard your prayer and seen your tears; I will heal you. On the third day from now you will go up to the temple of the Lord'." 2 Kings 20:5

"The Lord will sustain him on his sickbed and restore him from his bed of illness. I said, 'O Lord, have mercy on me; heal me, for I have sinned against you'." Psalm 41:3-4

"He heals the brokenhearted and binds up their wounds." Psalm 147:3

"There is a time for everything,...a time to kill and a time to heal, ..." Ecclesiastes 3:1, 3

"Jesus went through all the towns and villages, teaching in their synagogues, preaching the good news of the kingdom and healing every disease and sickness." Matthew 9:35

"Great crowds came to him, bringing the lame, the blind, the crippled, the mute and many others, and laid them at his feet; and he healed them." Matthew 15:30

"A large crowd followed and pressed around him. And a woman was there who had been subject to bleeding for twelve years. She had suffered a great deal under the care of many doctors and had spent all she had, yet instead of getting better she grew worse. When she heard about Jesus, she came up behind him in the crowd and touched his cloak, because she thought, 'If I just touch his clothes, I will be healed.' Immediately her bleeding stopped and she felt in her body that she was freed from her suffering.

At once Jesus realized that power had gone out from him. He turned around in the crowd and asked, 'Who touched my clothes?'

'You see the people crowding against you,' his disciples answered, 'and yet you can ask, 'Who touched me?'

But Jesus kept looking around to see who had done it. Then the woman, knowing what had happened to her, came and fell at his feet and, trembling with fear, told him the whole truth. He said to her, 'Daughter, your faith has healed you. Go in peace and be freed from your suffering'." Mark 5:24-34

"They drove out many demons and anointed many sick people with oil and healed them." Mark 6:13

"...but the crowds learned about it and followed him. He welcomed them and spoke to them about the kingdom of God, and healed those who needed healing." Luke 9:11

"One of them, when he saw he was healed came back, praising God in a loud voice." Luke 17:15

"When he heard this, Jesus said, 'This sickness will not end in death. No, it is for God's glory so that God's Son may be glorified through it'." John 11:4

"Is any one of you in trouble? He should pray. Is anyone happy? Let him sing songs of praise. Is any one of you sick? He should call the elders of the church to pray over him and anoint him with oil in the name of the Lord. And the prayer offered in faith will make the sick person well; the Lord will raise him up. If he has sinned, he will be forgiven. Therefore confess your sins to each other and pray for each other so that you may be healed. The prayer of a righteous man is powerful and effective." James 5:13-16

"Dear friend, I pray that you may enjoy good health and that all may go well with you, even as your soul is getting along well." 3 John 2

Prayer

God, we ask for Your healing to come to _____ (Name). S/he is sick and desperately needs Your healing touch. From the scriptures we have read, You clearly are the Great Physician, Who touches and heals us. You also heal through others and so we ask that healing come to _____ (Name) through the doctors and nurses and other health care persons who care for him/ her.

God, the verses from the Apostle James indicate that our prayer of faith will make sick people well. And so Lord we pray in that confidence that You will heal _____(Name). We believe in Your power to heal and we are assured that our faithful prayers are powerful and effective.

We thank You for the healing You are bringing to ____ (Name).

Joy

Anecdote

Vivian was surprised to see Janice looking so happy as she entered her living room.

"You look so happy today, have you had some good news?" Vivian asked.

"Oh yes I have. A year ago they told my daughter that she could never have a child. Today their son, Jonathan, was born—6 pounds 10 ounces and 21 inches long. He checks out perfectly normal!" Janice almost glowed.

"Oh Janice, that is wonderful news!" Vivian was thrilled with the news. "Do you remember that we prayed for your daughter last year? We asked God to give them a baby. You have been telling me that her pregnancy was going well. And now I'm almost as excited as you are!" Vivian gave Janice an enthusiastic hug.

"Since they phoned, I haven't been able to think about

anything else!" Janice smiled through her happy tears.

"Let's thank God for this great joy!" Vivian suggested.

Scriptures

"...as the time when the Jews got relief from their enemies, and as the month when their sorrow was turned into joy and their mourning into a day of celebration. He wrote them to observe the days as days of feasting and joy and giving presents of food to one another and gifts to the poor." Esther 9:22

"...weeping may remain for a night, but rejoicing comes in the morning." Psalm 30:5

"Let me hear joy and gladness; let the bones you have crushed rejoice....Restore to me the joy of your salvation and grant me a willing spirit, to sustain me." Psalm 51:8, 12

"Shout with joy to God, all the earth!" Psalm 66:1

"He settles the barren woman in her home as a happy mother of children." Psalm 113:9

"You will go out in joy and be led forth in peace; the mountains and hills will burst into song before you, and all the trees of the field will clap their hands." Isaiah 55:12

"...the sounds of joy and gladness, the voices of bride and bridegroom, and the voices of those who bring thank offerings to the house of the Lord, saying, 'Give thanks to the Lord almighty, for the Lord is good; his love endures forever'." Jeremiah 33:11

"When they saw the star they were overjoyed." Matthew 2:10

"He [Jesus] will be a joy and delight to you, and many will rejoice because of his birth..." Luke 1:14

"But the angel said to them, 'Do not be afraid, I bring you good news of great joy that will be for all the people'." Luke 2:10

"In the same way, I tell you, there is rejoicing in the presence of the angels of God over one sinner who repents'." Luke 15:10

"And the disciples were filled with joy and with the Holy Spirit." Acts 13:52

"But the fruit of the spirit is love, joy, peace, patience, kindness, goodness, faithfulness, gentleness and self-control." Galatians 5:22, 23

"In all my prayers for all of you, I always pray with joy...." Philippians 1:4

"Recalling your tears, I long to see you, so that I may be filled with joy." 2 Timothy 1:4

"Though you have not seen him, you love him; and even though you do not see him now, you believe in him and are filled with an inexpressible and glorious joy...." 1 Peter 1:8

Prayer

God, ____ (Name) is so grateful to You for the great joy You have brought to her family. Lord, we celebrate this occasion. We bow in humility realizing how you have answered our prayer for _____ (specific request).

God, this is the joy that You have given. We rejoice, Lord, for what You have given to us.

Peace

Anecdote

"I feel that I am in a whirlwind. I have so many appointments—doctor's office, therapy, treatments. I don't ever seem to get any rest," Patricia confided her state of mind.

"Pat, I know that you are very busy. I can't always find you at home when I call," Priscilla commented.

"Because I can't walk, it seems as if everything takes such a long time and when I get home I am exhausted," Pat sighed her frustration.

"Pat, your life is very complicated just now. Have you ever considered handing these burdens to God in exchange for His peace?"

"What do you mean—I don't understand?" Pat frowned.

"I will read some scriptures that focus on peace, and then we can talk about how you can experience this peace—even while you are going from place to place," Priscilla replied.

Scriptures

"The Lord turn his face toward you and give you peace." Numbers 6:26

"I will lie down and sleep in peace, for you alone, O Lord, make me dwell in safety." Psalm 4:8

"The Lord gives strength to his people; the Lord blesses his people with peace." Psalm 29:11

"Do not fret because of evil men or be envious of those who do wrong; for like the grass they will soon wither, like green plants they will soon die away. Trust in the Lord and do good; dwell in the land and enjoy safe pasture. Delight yourself in the Lord and he will give you the desires of your heart. Commit your way to the Lord; trust in him and he will do this: He will make your righteousness shine like the dawn, the justice of your cause like the noonday sun." Psalm 37:1-6

"Cast your cares on the Lord and he will sustain you; he will never let the righteous fall." Psalm 55:22

"Praise be to the Lord, to God our savior, who daily bears our burdens." Psalm 68:19

"I will listen to what God the Lord will say; he promises peace to his people, his saints – but let them not return to folly." Psalm 85:8

"'Peace I leave with you; my peace I give you. I do not give to you as the world gives. Do not let your hearts be troubled and do not be afraid'." John 14:27

"'I have told you these things, so that in me you may have peace. In this world you will have trouble. But take heart! I have overcome the world'." John 16:33

"Therefore, since we have been justified through faith, we have peace with God through our Lord Jesus Christ." Romans 5:1

"But the fruit of the spirit is love, joy, peace, patience, kindness, goodness, faithfulness, gentleness and self-control." Galatians 5:22-23

"Do not be anxious about anything, but in everything, present your requests to God. And the peace of God, which transcends all understanding, will guard your hearts and your minds in Christ Jesus." Philippians 4:6-7

"Now may the Lord of peace himself give you peace at all times and in every way." 2 Thessalonians 3:16

Prayer

God _____ (Name) is feeling unsettled due to _____ (reason). We ask that you will give a strong sense of Your peace to manage the activities of this day and to allow her/him to rest this night. God, we ask for that sense of turning over the worries and concerns to You.

God, we list the specific concerns now — (Describe details). Now, _____(Name) wants to release these burdens and leave them with You, knowing that You do Your work in Your way. While You are working, we ask that _____ (Name) can experience release from the burden and that release is followed by the restful flow of Your peace coursing through her/him.

Salvation

Anecdote

"From some of the church people who come to visit me I keep hearing words that I do not understand," Sonja frowned in her perplexity.

"What are the words you don't understand?" Melody, her visitor, asked. She knew that Sonja was a newcomer to the church and how frequently church jargon crept into any conversation.

"As I listened to the tape of the sermon, I heard the pastor mention *eternal life* the *gospel* and *salvation*. Those words are new to me. I've been to church all my life—before I became wheelchair bound—but I don't think I ever heard people mention those words," Sonja responded.

"Those words the pastor used are the basis of our belief," Melody began. "Let me try to explain this as simply as I can.

You know that when I visit—I often give you five or six things that you can think about until I return. Today, I'll give you seven words and define them in relation to scripture references that I'll write out so you can review them later," Melody said as she silently prayed that God's Spirit would help Sonja understand the gospel message.

God—We can have peace with God because He loves us.

"For God so loved the world that he gave his one and only Son, that whoever believes in him shall not perish but have eternal life." John 3:16

"Therefore, since we have been justified through faith, we have peace with God through our Lord Jesus Christ." Romans 5:1

Human beings—Are created in God's image and have autonomy.

"...to all who received him, to those who believed in his name, he gave the right to become children of God." John 1:12

Sin—Humans choose to do things in their own sinful way and these choices separate them from God.

"...for all have sinned and fall short of the glory of God,..." Romans 3:23

"For the wages of sin is death, but the gift of God is eternal life in Christ Jesus our Lord." Romans 6:23

Jesus—God's Son died on the cross to pay the penalty for our sins.

"In the beginning was the Word, and the Word was with God, and the Word was God. The Word became flesh and made his dwelling among us. We have seen his glory, the glory of the One and Only, who came from the Father, full of grace and truth." John 1:1, 14

"For God so loved the world that he gave his one and only Son, that whoever believes in him shall not perish but have eternal life." John 3:16

Response—Receive Christ by personal invitation to be saved from sin.

"Yet to all who received him, to those who believed in his name, he gave the right to become children of God." John 1:12

"...if you confess [state] with your mouth, 'Jesus is Lord,' and believe in your heart that God raised him from the dead, you will be saved." Romans 10:9

Faith—belief that Jesus' death paid the penalty for human sin and the cross on which He died bridges the gap created by human sin between God and humans. The belief that Jesus took on human sin and paid the penalty by His death is the only way humans can have their sins forgiven and be saved from eternal death. No good works or moral living can pay the human sin penalty.

"But God demonstrates his own love for us in this: While we were still sinners, Christ died for us." Romans 5:8

"Jesus answered, 'I am the way and the truth and the life. No one comes to the Father except through me'." John 14:6

"For it is by grace you have been saved, through faith—and this not from yourselves, it is the gift of God—not by works, so that no one can boast." Ephesians 2:8-9

Eternal Life—of the soul living in the Presence of God after bodily death.

"'I tell you the truth, whoever hears my word and believes him who sent me has eternal life and will not be condemned; he has crossed over from death to life'." John 5:24

"And this is the testimony: God has given us eternal life, and this life is in his Son. He who has the Son has life; he who does not have the Son of God does not have life. I write these things to you who believe in the name of the Son of God so that you may know that you have eternal life." 1 John 5:11-13

Anecdote

"These seven words are what are considered to be the *gospel* or good news to people because they can have forgiveness of their sin that allows them to have peace now and eternal life with God. Jesus' death on the cross, for all of human sin, paid the penalty that is required by a holy God," Melody paused. "Does this explain what is meant by some of the words you wondered about—*saved, salvation, gospel?*"

"Yes," Sonja replied obviously deep in thought. "I have never heard this explained like this before. I thought that God loved everyone. I didn't understand that human sin separated us from God. I've certainly sinned—probably more than my share."

"We all have sinned more than we would wish. But as a Christian, I can ask God to forgive me and then I can have His peace and love in my life," Melody replied. "Sonja, if you ever want to pray to ask God to take away sin through Jesus' death on the cross, anyone from church—Pastor _____ or I would be happy to pray with you."

Prayer

God, You honored the prayer recorded in the Bible when the man on the cross simply asked You to be merciful to him—to forgive his sins.

God, I ask that You forgive my sins. I believe that Jesus died on the cross to pay the penalty for all my sin. I want to personally accept this pardon and in faith believe that I have eternal life with God. Thank You for the wonderful sense of freedom from the burden of sin I have carried. Thank You for this new sense of Your peace and love in my life.

This is a basic prayer that can be adapted to fit specific situations. May have visitee repeat words after visitor reads them.

Suffering (Pain)

Anecdote

"I don't understand why God is leaving me here to suffer so much. They can't fix my back. I can't walk. Why doesn't God just take me?" Sam lamented.

"You are having to cope with a lot of pain," Pete said as he looked at the pain pump attached to Sam's arm.

"I think I'm a modern-day Job. My pain is unrelenting, even with this needle thing," Sam grimaced as he spoke.

"I recall that Job felt miserable and he expressed himself," Pete said as he reached for his handbook and flipped to the section on suffering. "I have Job's comments recorded in this book."

Scriptures

"Then Job replied: 'If only my anguish could be weighed and all my misery be placed on the scales! It would surely outweigh the sand of the seas—no wonder my words have been impetuous....Oh that I might have my request, that God would grant what I hope for, that God would be willing to crush me, to let loose his hand and cut me off'!" Job 6:1-2; 8-9

"Look upon my affliction and my distress and take away all my sins...." Psalm 25:18

"He will not let your foot slip—he who watches over you will not slumber." Psalm 121:3

"Why is my pain unending and my wound grievous and incurable?" Jeremiah 15:18

"Not only so, but we also rejoice in our sufferings, because we know that suffering produces perseverance; perseverance, character; and character, hope. And hope does not disappoint us, because God has poured out his love into our hearts by the Holy Spirit, whom he has given to us." Romans 5:3-5

"...for our light and momentary troubles are achieving for us an eternal glory that far outweighs them all." 2 Corinthians 4:17

"...there was given me a thorn in my flesh, a messenger of Satan, to torment me. Three times I pleaded with the Lord to take it away from me. But he said to me, 'My grace is sufficient for you, for my power is made perfect in weakness.' Therefore I will boast all the more gladly about my weaknesses, so that Christ's power may rest on me." 2 Corinthians 12:7-9

"For it is commendable if a man bears up under the pain of unjust suffering because he is conscious of God....But if you suffer for doing good and you endure it, this is commendable before God." 1 Peter 2:19-20

"And the God of all grace, who called you to his eternal glory in Christ, after you have suffered a little while, will himself restore you and make you strong, firm and steadfast." 1 Peter 5:10

"He will wipe away every tear from their eyes. There will be no more death or mourning or crying or pain, for the old order of things has passed away." Revelation 21:4

Prayer

God, _____(Name) is exhausted from this constant pain. I ask that You reach out Your Hand of love and ease his/her pain.

God, _____(Name) feels a lot like Job—unending pain that makes him desire death. God, please give of Your comfort—Your miracle of healing Lord.

Father, it seems too hard to even try to understand why _____ (Name) has such terrible suffering. I ask that You also give him/ her rest from all the questions and angry feelings that come with this unrelenting pain.

Assessment Review
Including Activities/Hobbies
(Designed to be used at Initial Visit)

Name_____   Phone_____

Address_____

Background:

Special Food or other Eating Needs _____

Food Preferences _____

What did you do for work? _____

What was your

      happiest experience?_____

      hardest experience? _____

What about

      past hobbies? _____

      current hobbies? _____

Activities visitor did with homebound person _____

_____

Other Information: _____

Form to be completed on initial visit and given to facilitator for filing. Copy of form to be given out when visitors change.

Visit Record Sheet should be attached with the following information:

Date	Hobby or Activity	Response of Visitee (1-low to 5-High)

Appendix C

Guidelines for Special Needs Arising in Visits to the Homebound

The purpose of making visits is to convey Christian love and extend the church community when the person or family cannot attend church. The focus usually includes socialization and encouragement in gracious spiritual areas—providing church bulletins and news, sharing scripture verses and prayer.

When dealing with people who are ill or who have physical disabilities, other physical and emotional needs may also arise. These guidelines are offered to provide direction for dealing with selected needs that may be requests from the homebound person (visitee) or family members or observed by the visitor and immediately reported to the Visitor Facilitator or Coordinator.

Legal Documents

Note the following areas that are not part of the homebound visitor role:

1. Do not sign any checks.
2. Do not initiate setting up Advanced Directives.
3. Do not work with Power of Attorney planning.
4. Do not assist with medical insurance details and other payment activities for setting up Medicaid or any other type of payment for services.

If needs in this area arise:

1. Contact Visitor Facilitator.
2. Family contact may be made after consultation with facilitator.

Transportation

1. Refer request to church office. Secretary will provide caller with a list of people who have volunteered to provide assistance. Person needing assistance is encouraged to pay for gas.
2. Review options with visitee to obtain assistance from family members, neighbors and others.
3. Discuss available public transportation—Wheelchair accommodation may be available with more specialized transportation services.

Change of Residence Need

1. Do not suggest that the visitee needs to move to a different type of care facility, but notify Visitor Facilitator about need observed.
2. If visitee asks for help in changing residence, contact Visitor Facilitator.

Abuse Situation

1. On observing or hearing about physical, mental or spiritual abuse, contact Visitor Facilitator immediately. In some cases the facilitator may ask for your assistance in writing up a report to be submitted to appropriate agency.
2. Be aware that sometimes visitee may be confused and some comments may be imagined rather than real. It may still be necessary to report these to the Visitor Facilitator.

Assisting with Physical Needs in Care Facility

In a care facility the visitor should only visit and not provide other assistance. Visitors should check with care personnel before even offering water.

Assisting with Physical Needs in Home Situation

The focus for the visitor is to communicate and socialize in a friendly way—reading, writing letter etc. but not sweeping the floor or doing other general house care activities.

When physical needs requiring trips to grocery, pharmacy, doctor or other places are requested the visitor should tell the person that transportation is available from the church office.

Assistance with meals is available through "Meals on Wheels".

As additional needs arise the Visit Facilitator should be contacted.

Major Decisions

Major health care and personal decisions should be referred to family members and facilitator.

Discussion of issues such as different or changes in treatments should be managed very carefully so that visitee does not get the impression that visitor is advising. Usually these would be referred to family.

Visitor should refrain from stating personal opinions on health care related issues. Words used should be chosen carefully. Do not make statements such as "you should" do such and such.

In any visit situation maintaining confidentiality is key. Caution should be used in bringing up prayer concerns to another group.

Initiation of a Homebound Visiting Ministry

A homebound visiting ministry is a source of encouragement to persons in a faith community when they are not physically able to be part of the gatherings in the worship place. The person responsible for working with senior members is typically the one who initiates this ministry, but anyone who identifies a need can check with the pastoral staff and with approval begin such a ministry. If a parish nurse is on the faith community's staff, she/he may initiate a community member visitation ministry.

A bulletin announcement usually draws people with a sense of compassion and caring who would be willing to visit the homebound. Materials included in this Handbook would be helpful to use as orientation material. For example Appendix C contains Guidelines for Special Needs Arising in Visits to the Homebound.

A monthly meeting is good for visitors to share particular challenges and needs that can be prayed for at the meeting. The Visitor Facilitator may need to modify a given visitor's assignment. One of the chapters of this workbook could be used as the focus for the remaining time.

The visitors need to know whom to call should something unusual occur on the visit. They should be encouraged to talk about church activities, being sure to include some newsy and light events too—not only a listing of those ill and persons who may have died. If bulletins are not mailed, these could be given to the homebound person. Sometimes the sanctuary flowers may be available to divide up for homebound people. Visitors might be encouraged to read scripture and to pray with their visitees.

Initially, it may be helpful to go on visits in pairs. A woman should not visit a male visitee without taking someone along with her. When two visit, the conversation usually is easier. The visitors need to focus on the needs of the visitees, particularly with respect to the length of the visit. Sometimes the visitee is unable to carry on conversation easily or may be too ill to talk for long. Usually 30-45 minutes is an acceptable time for a visit, unless the homebound person appears to be weary.

Because visiting requires so much personal investment of time and energy, the volunteer visitors need to be encouraged and prayed for by the faith community. After a year visitor assignments usually should be changed. An appreciation luncheon should be planned for the homebound visitors annually.

Obtaining Visitees

On initiating a church Visiting Group a logical question arises: "How do you get people to visit?" One easy way is to put a note in the church bulletin asking those who cannot come to services to call the church office to ask for a visitor.

Usually the Pastor to Seniors can provide a list of people who are homebound and would enjoy having someone from the church visit them. When the committee is publicized others in the church may contact the committee members with names of people who would like visits. Sometimes homebound people call the church office on their own and ask to have someone visit them.

If the church has a "Nineties Club" that is composed of persons who are ninety years old and older some of these may have limited mobility and be unable to get to church. Members of this group might be asked if they would like someone from the church to visit them.

Visiting Persons with Dementia
(Alzheimer's Disease)

In a small handbook such as this it is not possible to include a focus on every illness. But with such a large percentage developing various types of dementia that are often referred to as "Alzheimer's Disease," a brief comment on interacting with them is essential.

The most important point is to try to assess the level of confusion the person has developed and then gear the activities according to the ability of the person to focus, even if it is only for a brief time. For example, a visitor may choose to read scripture. While the visitee is reading, check to see if the visitee is comprehending and following or becoming restless and asking unrelated questions. Keeping any activity brief is essential because a confused visitee's attention span is usually short.

Another point is to relate to the visitee as an adult rather than as a child. Because words and activities often need to be simple, there is a tendency to move to child-like words and actions. But the visitee is not a child and typically becomes distressed when addressed in a childish manner.

Taking an assessment of the person's hobbies, often from another family member's perspective, is essential because the visitee is unable to recall previous interests and leisure pursuits. If, for example, the person enjoyed bird-watching in previous more active years, this might be a time to put a bird-feeder on the window sill. On seeing birds come to the window, the visitee might respond as in previous times and even talk about the birds and name them.

Even if music was not a special interest, the visitee may still respond when music is played and may sing along with well known songs and hymns from the past. Music may be helpful for the caregiver too. Visitors need to talk to both the person with mental confusion and the caregiver. Both need to be included in the conversation. The confused person may act out if he/she has a sense of being ignored with respect to the music or other aspects of conversation.

If your visitee is not able to carry on a conversation and respond due to some mental confusion or dementia, the visitor may want to review some books or articles.

Examples follow:

"Carved in Sand: When Attention Fails and Memory Fades in Midlife." Ramin, Cathryn Jakobson. New York: Harper Collins, 2006.

"Social Disconnectedness, Perceived Isolation, and Health Among Older Adults." Cornwell, Erin York and Linda J. Waite. *Journal of Health and Social Behavior* 2009. 50(1):31-48.

"What Are Friends For? A Longer Life." Tara Parker-Pope: *The New York Times,* April 20, 2009. Accessed on-line 2/24/12 at http://www.nytimes.com/2009/04/21/health/21well.html/

CPSIA information can be obtained
at www.ICGtesting.com
Printed in the USA
FFOW01n0844170318
45699702-46541FF

9 780988 146235